PATRIOT'S CHOICE

The Story of John Hancock

Also by Frederick Wagner

SUBMARINE FIGHTER OF THE AMERICAN REVOLUTION
The Story of David Bushnell

FAMOUS UNDERWATER ADVENTURERS

FAMOUS AMERICAN ACTORS AND ACTRESSES
(with Barbara Brady)

PATRIOT'S CHOICE

The Story of John Hancock

By FREDERICK WAGNER

ILLUSTRATED

DODD, MEAD & COMPANY

NEW YORK

Third Printing

Copyright © 1964 by Frederick Wagner
All rights reserved
No part of this book may be reproduced in any form
without permission in writing from the publisher
Library of Congress Catalog Card Number: 64-18658

Printed in the United States of America
by The Cornwall Press, Inc., Cornwall, N.Y.

Grateful acknowledgment is made for permission to use brief quotations as follows: on pages 40, 41, 141, 142, and 153 from the Massachusetts Society *Proceedings*, Third Series, Volumes XLIII and LX, reprinted by permission of the Massachusetts Historical Society; on pages 82, 86, and 101 from *Diary and Autobiography of John Adams*, Edited by L. H. Butterfield, Leonard C. Faber and Wendell D. Barrett, Cambridge, Mass.: The Belknap Press of Harvard University Press, Copyright, 1961, by Massachusetts Historical Society, reprinted by permission of the publishers; on page 90 from *The Writings of Samuel Adams*, collected and edited by Harry Alonzo Cushing, Copyright, 1906, by G. P. Putnam's Sons, reprinted by permission of G. P. Putnam's Sons; and on page 139 from *Letters of Members of the Continental Congress*, Volume I, August 29, 1774 to July 4, 1776, Edited by Edmund C. Burnett, published 1921 by the Carnegie Institution of Washington (Institution Publication No. 299), reprinted by permission of the Carnegie Institution of Washington.

For Jennifer and Jack

Acknowledgments

Once again I am deeply indebted to librarians in a number of towns and cities who have shown limitless patience in helping me gather material. In particular, I owe a special word of thanks to the staff of the Rare Book Room of the Boston Public Library, to various members of the staff of the Library of Congress, and to the staff of the Central Building of The New York Public Library—especially those in the American History and the Local History and Genealogy Rooms. I am also indebted to Stephen T. Riley, Director, Massachusetts Historical Society; to Thomas N. Maytham, Assistant in the Department of Paintings, and Drika N. Agnew of the Museum of Fine Arts, Boston; and to W. Edward Boughton of the John Hancock Mutual Life Insurance Company. To my editor, Joe Ann Daly, and to my wife, Barbara, I am grateful for patience and forbearance.

Wherever I had access to primary source material, I have, in using quotations, followed the spelling and punctuation—however capricious—of the original.

FREDERICK WAGNER

Contents

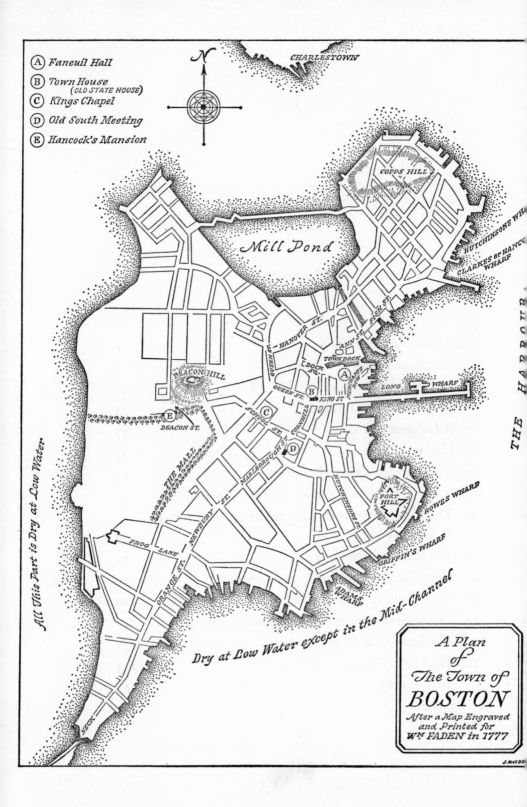

A Plan
of
The Town of
BOSTON
After a Map Engraved
and Printed for
Wᵐ FADEN in 1777

Illustrations

I

Parson Hancock's Son

For the town of Boston in the Province of Massachusetts Bay, the year 1744 had dawned quietly enough, but by May the wharves, the markets, the countinghouses all were astir with rumors. The latest trading vessels to drop anchor, battered by storm-tossed seas on the long voyage from England, carried word that still another war with France was about to erupt. Even the most peace-loving citizens of this hot-blooded town knew in their hearts that the next ship, or the one after, would bring news that the smoke of battle was again drifting across Europe.

To proud and portly Thomas Hancock, merchant extraordinary, sitting in his splendid stone mansion on Beacon Hill at the very outskirts of town, the rumors promised a mixed blessing. War made trade even more hazardous than usual. French ships, based in Canada or the West Indies, were likely to swoop down on his fine brigs and carry off their cargoes as prizes for King Louis XV. But war also promised profits, lucrative contracts to provision the garrisons in the New World manned by the soldiers of King George II of England.

In peace or war, Thomas Hancock knew how to drive a shrewd bargain, and although he was sometimes unlucky, he was rarely outmaneuvered.

Ten miles south of Boston, in the home of Thomas's elder brother, the Reverend Mr. Hancock of the north precinct of Braintree, little thought was given to war or rumors of war. The minister's family had too much trouble right at hand to pay much heed to the world outside. Early in May, after much "pining sickness and pain," the Reverend Mr. Hancock, aged forty-two, had died, leaving his widow little money and three small children to provide for.

Now, in an upstairs bedroom of the parsonage, a boy of seven stood aching with misery, watching his mother pack his clothes into a trunk. It was a small trunk, but large enough to hold everything he owned. A minister's son was not expected to be rich in worldly possessions.

At last, without a word, the boy turned and fled from the room, down the steep, crooked staircase, and out the front door. Stumbling, his eyes half-blinded by the tears that he struggled to hold back, he followed the path leading around to the rear of the house and on to the field where the lime trees grew. He was tempted to climb up into the branches to gaze across the gently rolling hills of Braintree toward the bay. Beyond the bay lay Boston, and his future.

He wandered farther from the parsonage, toward the church, his father's church, where his father would never preach again. The meetinghouse, built twelve years before, was the center of the village, and it had been the center of his own life. Shaped like a large wooden box, with a steeple towering aloft and a weather vane atop the steeple, it had always seemed a grand building, if one could overlook the bitterly cold drafts of winter and the stifling heat of summer. There, a little more than seven years before, the Reverend Mr. Hancock had baptized his first son, four days old, recording the ceremony in the church annals: "John Hancock, my son." The boy's birthday had been January 23, 1737.

Young John slipped inside for a last look around. Directly across from the door was the pulpit where, every Sunday, morning and afternoon, his father had preached his sermons, which sometimes lasted as long as four hours. In his mind John still could hear his father's deep baritone ringing out, reminding his congregation of the liberties they enjoyed under the English constitution, and the special privileges they possessed under the Massachusetts charter. Even for a boy of seven, it was a lesson not quickly forgotten.

From the pulpit, now looming huge in its emptiness, the Reverend Mr. Hancock had looked out upon the congregation, his family in the pew on his left, Deacon Adams's family in the pew on the right. In this pew young John Adams, slightly more than a year older than John Hancock, fidgeted through the sermons—when he was not sitting with the swarming hive of whispering boys up in the gallery that stretched around three sides of the meetinghouse.

Parson Hancock knew everyone in his congregation, man, woman and child; master, servant and slave; sinner, sinned against and saint. He shared their joy when crops were good, their sorrow when crops failed. The town of 1,500 people was widely scattered, the houses spread out along the Coast Road, but in the Hancock meetinghouse they all became one close, tightly knit family. Ever since John could remember, these Sunday meetings had made him proud of the way his father watched over everyone. It was something to live up to.

Before turning to leave the meetinghouse, he paused for a moment beside the pew held by the leading citizen of Braintree, Colonel Quincy. The Quincys had always filled him with awe, but John little suspected how importantly the Quincy clan would figure in his life. Three years from now, a daughter would be born to the wife of one of Colonel Quincy's sons. This girl was destined to become Mrs. John Hancock.

Once outside the church, John trudged across the road to the burying ground, unfenced, open to the highway. Slightly apart from the other graves was the Ministers' Tomb, where the Reverend Mr. Hancock had been buried a short time ago.

His father would not have wanted him to cry in public, and John struggled not to. In Braintree, as the parson's son, he had been expected to set an example, to live up to what his father wanted him to be. It had not been easy. Many a time he had envied the other boys—his friend John Adams, for example— whose fathers were merely good, staunch farmers. The eyes of Braintree were not always watching them.

But John Hancock had been happy. He had roamed the fields and hills; he had wandered along the creeks and in the swamps. In the summer he had sailed kites from Penn's hill, and in the winter he had joined the crowd of shouting boys sledding down the icy slopes.

And even schooldays had been fun, in Dame Belcher's house farther down the Coast Road, near the Adams's farm. The single room set aside for the school had been crowded, and Dame Belcher's mode of teaching had been delightfully free and easy. By now John knew how to read and write, and he also knew a bit about working ciphers. Whatever Dame Belcher lacked as a pedagogue (and she lacked a great deal), John's father had provided. Nearly every evening John would gather around the parsonage fireside with his sister and brother, Mary and Eben, to listen to their father's lessons. Parson Hancock could be much sterner than Dame Belcher, and he taught them well.

Turning away from the burying ground, John ran down the road toward the parsonage. Today was packing day, and there was no time for a visit with Dame Belcher. The Hancocks were making ready to say good-bye to Braintree.

John's mother, for the time being at least, would stay with his grandfather, who had been the pastor at Lexington for nearly half a century, a burly and beloved old man with flashing black eyes and a wit that could strike like lightning. With her would go nine-year-old Mary and little Ebenezer, not yet three. And John—John was to go to Boston, to live with Uncle Thomas and Aunt Lydia Hancock on Beacon Hill.

His mother insisted that this was a stroke of good fortune, yet John viewed the prospect gloomily. It was heart-breaking to lose his father. Now he was to be torn away from his mother and sister and brother. Uncle Thomas, by his sheer bulk, was a rather frightening and forbidding personage, and Aunt Lydia was equally massive. How could he be happy with them?

But Uncle Thomas wanted an heir to carry on his flourishing mercantile empire, and he and his wife were childless. Mary was a girl and would not do. Eben was too small to be separated from his mother. John remained the only candidate, and John had been chosen. Moreover, he was the elder son, just as his father had been an elder son, and in eigheenth-century New England the first-born male in a family was accorded greater privileges than any sons who followed.

By the time John reached the parsonage, the packing had been completed. It was almost time to go. Frightening though it might be, a great adventure was starting.

II

Merchant Hancock's Nephew

The coach that bore Master Hancock to Boston had a rough road to follow. In 1744 the only land route to Boston was by way of the village of Roxbury and "The Neck," a narrow isthmus scarcely forty yards broad. The marshy roadbed lay so low that it was frequently washed by spring tides, and during storms it was swept by sea spray.

Travel in eighteenth-century America offered few comforts and a good many jolts and bumps, but John paid little attention to the hardships of the journey. As the coach carried him through unfamiliar hamlets and villages, the sorrow over leaving Braintree grew less intense with each new milestone. Excitement took its place, an excitement that even the desolate, unpaved track across "The Neck" did not diminish. Barren as the roadway was, it led to the thriving town of Boston, the town where his Uncle Thomas was a man of great importance.

Just outside the town gate he stared with a horrified fascination at a grim sight: piles of stones marking the graves of criminals and, standing in the midst of them, the town gallows.

John shuddered and drew back from the coach window, never dreaming that one day he would be threatened with hanging from the very gallows that now loomed so stark and terrifying in the mist from the sea.

Through the town gate and on down Orange Street and Newbury Street he went, and then, as the coach rounded a corner, the Common burst upon his eyes. For more than a century this splendid tract, forty-five rolling green acres stretching to the farthest edge of the west end of town, had been a common ground for the citizens of Boston. It served as a training field for the militia, a pasture for cows and sheep, a watering place for horses. Across the southeast corner was a pleasant mall formed by two rows of trees, and here, in the afternoon after teatime, the gallants of the town would stroll with their ladies. Perhaps the most prominent landmark on the Common was the great elm from whose branches three Quakers had been hanged. The deed had been done nearly a century before John Hancock rode into town, but it had not been forgotten.

As the coach rattled over the cobblestones of the snarled and twisting streets, John gazed with awe. With 17,000 inhabitants, Boston was by far the largest town in the colonies. Philadelphia had only 13,000 citizens, and New York a mere 11,000. Now that King George's War had broken out, all Boston was astir with preparations. Soldiers were collecting for proposed expeditions; privateers were making ready at the wharves. Even the constant ringing of bells—church bells and street bells—could not drown out the din of men making ready to go to battle.

The coach turned off to the left, and there, on the south slope near the crest of Beacon Hill, sat the imposing mansion of Thomas Hancock, completed in all its magnificence the year that John had been born. On the summit of the hill stood the tall mast that gave Beacon Hill its name. Near the top of this mast was a crane from which a massive iron skillet was suspended, designed to hold a barrel of tar or other combustibles. When lighted, the beacon could be seen far inland, an alarm to the countryside that Massachusetts Bay was being invaded.

Standing on a lot more than 135 feet broad and 300 feet deep (to which Thomas Hancock shrewdly added every time he could purchase more land), the Hancock house was built of granite from the Braintree quarries and planned to last for centuries. Two stories high, surmounted by a tiled gambrel roof, the house had more than fifty windows from which merchant Hancock could survey his domain and the surrounding countryside.

"Its Allowed on all hands," he wrote to a friend, "the Kingdom of England don't afford so fine a Prospect as I have both of Land and Water."

His grounds were indeed beautiful; Mr. Thomas Hancock was not a man to stint expense where the grandeur of his living was concerned. The flower beds, carefully tended, were bordered by box imported from England. And there were other shrubs and trees brought from across the sea—walnut, mulberry, cherry, pear, plum, peach, apricot, gooseberry. No wonder Hancock boasted that England did not afford so fine a prospect: he believed he had taken the finest that England had to offer.

The coach, spattered with mud from its trip across "The Neck," drew to a halt before the low stone wall surrounding the Hancock grounds. John hopped out, ran up the paved walk, and climbed the dozen stone steps leading to the front door, where Uncle Thomas and Aunt Lydia waited to welcome him.

They were a formidable pair. Aunt Lydia, just past thirty, had the appearance of an overgrown pug-dog, and John could not keep from staring at the large wart above her right eyebrow. Even her husband, when ordering a carriage from London, had been forced to admit, "Mrs. Hancock is none of the shortest and smallest of folks, though I'd prefer as light a one as possible to her size." But she was gracious, good, and God-fearing, and although she loved to manage other people's lives, she usually managed them for the better.

At forty-one, Thomas Hancock was stout and stern, with a full wig, full face, double chin, and sharp-sighted dark eyes. Not much escaped his notice. He had made his way to Boston at the age of fourteen, while John's father was studying for the ministry at Harvard College. After serving out a seven-year apprenticeship to a local bookseller, he was able to scrape together enough money to open his own bookstore at the sign of "The Bible and Three Crowns," in Drawbridge Street near the Town Dock.

He was as fortunate in his friendships as in his business dealings. One of his friends was Daniel Henchman, a thriving bookbinder and bookseller, and in 1730, at the age of twenty-seven, Thomas married Daniel's daughter Lydia, who had just reached sixteen.

Once Thomas had allied himself with Lydia (and, incidentally, with the Henchman money), his rise was swift. Soon books were only a small part of his stock in trade. He imported tea, coffee, paper, glass, ribbons and cloth, and his goal was profit for himself rather than profit for the London merchants from whom he bought his goods. Among his exports were whalebones and oil, lumber, salt fish, pork, cattle, horses. He began to buy ships, or shares in ships, and soon craft such as the brig *Charming Lydia* were plying a triangular course between Boston and the West Indies and Holland, or between Boston and Newfoundland and England. When ready cash was short (and it usually was), Hancock and the other merchants resorted to the barter system, selling goods in exchange for other goods.

As a prospering general merchant, Thomas Hancock found himself assuming other functions. At times his ships provided passage for travelers to and from England. He acted as banker for friends and business associates. He encouraged local farmers to spend the long winter evenings making bowls and buckets and ax handles; as local industry increased, so did his source of exports.

Not all of his activities would bear close scrutiny. Along with other colonial merchants, he felt that the Navigation Acts passed by Parliament imposed unfair duties. In protest (at least he justified his deeds as a protest), he instructed his ship captains to smuggle contraband past the customs inspectors. Other New Englanders did the same, and the practice increased as the decades passed.

It was also rumored around Boston that some of the Hancock vessels—exactly how many no one was ever quite sure—had suddenly appeared on the high seas as privateers, only to reappear in Boston harbor as peaceful trading ships.

With the outbreak of King George's War, Thomas Hancock found a new way to increase the scope of his legitimate activities. Through the influence of his London agent, he and another Boston merchant garnered the contracts to supply the British garrisons in Newfoundland and at Annapolis Royal in Nova Scotia. It was a lucrative business, and undoubtedly Thomas still was gloating over his good fortune the day he welcomed his small nephew to the Hancock mansion.

After the Spartan simplicity of the parsonage in Braintree, John was dazzled by the opulence of his Uncle Thomas's home. As he was led through the hall toward the broad staircase, he caught only a glimpse of the drawing room and dining hall to the right and the family parlor to the left. The wallpaper, ordered from London, was decorated with fruit, flowers, peacocks, macaws, squirrels and monkeys. John had never seen anything so splendid. Equally dazzling were the four bedrooms on the second floor, with their fittings of crimson or yellow damask and their stately canopied fourposters.

Later, exploring the house, John discovered the other rooms on the first floor: a smaller dining room generally used by the family, a china room, a library and office. From the rear of the main entrance hall a door opened out to the garden and summer house, with the coach house and barn beyond.

As soon as possible Uncle Thomas carried John off for a tour of the wharves, stores and offices that made up the Hancock empire. By far the finest wharf in town was the Long Wharf, in which he owned shares. Built in 1710, this superb pier extended nearly 2,000 feet out into the bay. Along the whole length of the north side of the pier were shops, warehouses and sail lofts, and the far end was fortified. The south side was left clear for the passage of horses, carts and people.

It was a fascinating place, with almost a carnival atmosphere. Curiosities were frequently on display—figures modeled in wax, or a polar bear, or even a pirate's head, carefully preserved in brine. Forming a colorful backdrop were the sailing ships at anchor in the harbor.

From Long Wharf Thomas hustled his nephew over to Clark's Wharf, not far away. The shrewd merchant had already begun buying shares in this thriving pier, and by 1761 he would own seven-eighths of the property. Even though he renamed it Hancock's Wharf, Bostonians were slow to change their habits; many of the townspeople persisted in calling it Clark's Wharf until long after Thomas Hancock's death.

This day a swarm of boys gathered on the wharf to glimpse the country boy who had the good fortune to live with wealthy merchant Hancock. Among them was Paul Revere, the nine-year-old son of a French silversmith whose shop and home were near the head of the wharf. Paul eyed the Hancock lad without envy. Obviously, Boston's most prospering merchant would never allow his nephew the freedom that Revere

himself enjoyed, freedom to roam the cobblestone streets or
dive from the wharves. The two boys seemed headed along
totally different paths, and neither one dreamed that thirty
years later they would be traveling a path together—the road
to liberty.

In the days that followed the visit to the wharf, Uncle
Thomas made certain that John explored all the landmarks of
the town—Faneuil Hall with its market, the Town House and
the Province House, Old South Church and Old North
Church. And there were frequent visits to the parsonage at
Lexington, where John's mother and Mary and Eben were
staying with old Reverend Hancock. These were joyful trips,
but as the weeks and months passed, John's ties to his mother
loosened. He began to feel that he belonged in Boston, that he
belonged with Uncle Thomas and Aunt Lydia. There the very
air seemed charged with excitement.

The spring of 1745 brought a martial pageant right to John's
doorstep. One morning, looking out toward the Common, he
saw a milling throng of soldiers, 3,000 in all, setting up camp
on the rolling green acres. All the slaves and servants in the
Beacon Hill mansion were agog with excitement, and the
master of the household, Merchant Hancock, could not restrain a smile at the thought of the additional profits that came
with each new campaign.

The Governor of Massachusetts was about to undertake a
bold campaign against Louisbourg, the French stronghold on
Cape Breton Island. Known as the Gibraltar of America,
Louisbourg commanded the approaches to the Gulf of St.
Lawrence—and to French-held Canada. It seemed foolhardy,
John heard some of his uncle's friends say, for a force of New
England men to attempt to bring the French to their knees.
And these were New England men alone. The only assistance
to be lent by England herself was a single squadron from the
Royal Navy.

When the troops marched off to battle in March, drums beating and fifes playing, John cheered them on lustily. Then, for weeks, little news was heard, and the boy almost forgot a campaign was being waged.

But about four o'clock in the morning of July 3 he was startled from sleep by the sound of gunfire, beating drums, and the ringing of church bells. Dashing downstairs he found his uncle already in the main hall, talking with one of the town militia who had rushed up from the waterfront with momentous news. An express packet had just dropped anchor in the harbor, bearing dispatches telling of a great victory. More than two weeks earlier the mighty fortress at Louisbourg had capitulated. New England men had proved their worth—without help from the British Army.

No business was done in Boston that day, not even at Hancock's store, The Bible and Three Crowns. Each man tried to outdo his neighbor in celebrating, and in the evening the whole town "appeared as it were in a Blaze, almost every House being finely illluminated." There were fireworks in the streets and bonfires in the fields, and on the Common was the most splendid bonfire of all. That night, in the great house on Beacon Hill, Thomas Hancock played host at a sumptuous victory banquet.

From the window of his upstairs bedroom, John watched the carriages arrive, and until late into the night he could hear the distant sound of voices and laughter. Outside, a crowd lined the lane in front of the house, watching what they could of the festivities within. John never forgot the way the people cheered when his uncle sent out a servant to distribute coins by the handful. He was sure that no man in Boston that night was more popular than his uncle.

A few days after the Louisbourg celebration, John enrolled in Boston's oldest and most famous school, the Public Latin School, also known as the South Grammar. A one-story building, scarcely large enough to hold the hard benches to seat a hundred pupils, it stood on School Street next to King's Chapel. The famous clergyman, Cotton Mather, had studied there, as had Benjamin Franklin. And other graduates of South Grammar were soon to make their mark, among them the cousin of John Adams of Braintree—Samuel Adams, at this moment a disgruntled clerk in a countinghouse, who gave little indication of his future political brilliance.

First as usher, then as master, John Lovell had reigned at the South Grammar for nearly thirty years when John Hancock entered, and he was to reign for thirty years more. Just recently, in delivering the funeral oration for Peter Faneuil (who had the misfortune to die almost as soon as he had finished building Faneuil Hall), Lovell had made a statement that time would underline with irony: "May Liberty always spread its joyful wings over this place. May Loyalty to a king under whom we enjoy that Liberty ever remain our character."

Loyalty to the king remained Lovell's character. When war came in 1775, he closed school, so tradition says, with the comment, "Put away your books. War's begun, and school's done." And with other Loyalists he sailed away from Boston, to die in Halifax, a lonely, broken-hearted old man.

But in 1745 loyalty to the king was the rule in Boston, not the exception, and Lovell managed his students with a hand and tongue that could strike terror. School started at seven in the morning (eight during the winter) and lasted until five in the afternoon. Vacations were short and infrequent, a week at Thanksgiving and Christmas, and three weeks during the summer. The rest of the year the boys worked hard, concentrating most of their efforts on Latin, Greek and penmanship. Although no records have survived to show how John fared at Latin and Greek, his famous signature is eloquent testimony that he excelled at penmanship.

During these years at school it seemed to John that Boston

was constantly in an uproar. In 1746 the entire countryside became alarmed by rumors that a French squadron was sailing toward the coast. With an attack expected daily, more than 6,000 armed men flocked into town and set up camp on the Common. But storms at sea caught and destroyed the enemy squadron, and the countrymen on the Common went back to their farms, shops, smithies and taverns.

The following year the British themselves roused Boston to fury by tampering with the rights of her citizens. Commodore Charles Knowles, commanding a number of men-of-war in Boston Harbor, emerged as the villain of the incident. When his seamen began deserting in increasing numbers, Knowles sent a press gang ashore to seek them out. Instead of apprehending the deserters, the press gang carried off several Boston apprentices and laborers from the wharves.

Boston was always quick to anger, and on this November day a mob gathered with the speed of lightning. Armed with sticks, mops, clubs, and rusty swords, the leaderless swarm of Bostonians seized one of Knowles's lieutenants as a hostage. After roaming restlessly through the streets all day, soon after dusk the mob approached the Town House—later to be called the Old State House—and began hurling bricks through the windows of the chamber where the provincial legislature, the General Court, was sitting. In an effort to stem the wave of their fury, the Royal Governor, William Shirley, stepped out on the balcony to swear that he would do everything he could to have the impressed Bostonians set free.

Commodore Knowles stubbornly refused to cooperate. By the next day the captives had not been given their liberty, and the mob still wandered through the town. The militia was called out, but showed little inclination to interfere with the muttering crowds in the streets. Governor Shirley, fearing that the mob might turn on him for failing to make headway with Knowles, escaped by boat to Castle William, a fort on an island in the bay. Knowles, flying into a rage over the fact that the Royal Governor had been forced to retreat, now threatened to bombard the town.

With bombardment and bloodshed imminent, Thomas Hancock and other responsible citizens hastily called a town meeting, in an attempt to restore order and law to the strife-torn community. Townspeople were required to attend these meetings, which wielded considerable authority in local government. This town meeting achieved what the Royal Governor could not achieve. The mob broke up; reason prevailed; and a tide of calm spread through Boston. To avoid a new outburst, Knowles agreed to release the men he had seized; Governor Shirley came back from the haven of Castle William. The Bostonians congratulated themselves; they had shown the Royal Navy that their liberties were not to be trifled with.

After the insurrection, Governor Shirley never trusted the temper of the Province of Massachusetts Bay. And time after time he sent letters back to England warning that the Boston town meeting, with its control over the affairs of the town, would eventually prove a source of trouble. Parliament—to its eventual regret—paid little attention to his warnings.

Meanwhile, in the great mansion on Beacon Hill, John Hancock was growing up. Although Uncle Thomas and Aunt Lydia doted upon him, they expected far too much to allow him to be spoiled. After all, if he was to inherit the vast mercantile empire that Uncle Thomas had built up, he would have to be worthy of the honor. And when Aunt Lydia allowed herself the luxury of daydreams, she foresaw other honors in store for her handsome young nephew—perhaps a knighthood, perhaps even an appointment as Royal Governor of the Province of Massachusetts Bay.

III

Master John Hancock of Harvard

In 1748 the Peace of Aix-la-Chapelle brought to a close the
War of the Austrian Succession in Europe and King George's
War in America. The terms of the treaty outraged even such
a loyal subject of King George II as Thomas Hancock (who
never felt that his smuggling had anything to do with loyalty
or disloyalty).

Young John listened wide-eyed as his uncle stumped back
and forth in the mansion on Beacon Hill, yelping with pain
from his gouty leg and snorting with indignation over the way
New England had been dealt with by Old England. According to the peace treaty, Louisbourg—the prize captured by
New England initiative and New England men—was to be
returned to France by England in exchange for Madras in
India. Who, Hancock growled, had ever heard of Madras?
And what Massachusetts man gave a farthing for it? Louisbourg was what counted, and now Louisbourg had been
snatched away. It was beginning to dawn upon Merchant
Hancock, as it was upon other men in the Province, that the

best interests of England were not always the best interests of New England.

Thomas Hancock had other things to complain about than his gout and the loss of Louisbourg. With the coming of peace, trade slowed down, and a postwar depression set in. Prices plummeted, and in the months that followed he found that goods were piling up on the shelves of his stores—and staying there. His voice re-echoed throughout the house as he thundered that ruin was almost upon him.

But ruin was far from imminent. It would take more than a depression to undermine the mercantile empire that he had forged, and when legitimate trading became stagnant, he turned again to smuggling.

His operations as a smuggler did not prevent Uncle Thomas from playing an increasingly important role as a respectable citizen in the town meeting, which New Englanders regarded as the very bedrock of their freedom. Although the real legislative power lay with the Governor and the General Court (composed of a Governor's Council and a House of Representatives), the town meeting exerted a strong influence. The townspeople were urged to air their grievances and discuss their problems in these public forums, and although the wealthier obviously had more influence, the town meeting was remarkably democratic. One of the committees on which Hancock served was appointed to petition the General Court to remove a duty laid on tea, coffee, coaches, chaises and other articles. It is easy to understand why this particular task was one the merchant undertook with special fervor; it touched upon matters close to his heart and his pocketbook.

While Uncle Thomas was combining his roles as smuggler and town father, Aunt Lydia's father, Daniel Henchman, embarked on a venture as hazardous as Thomas's running of contraband. Parliament had forbidden the printing of the Scriptures anywhere in the colonies, yet Henchman had apparently grown weary of publishing such volumes as *A compleat Body of Divinity* (in 914 double-column pages) and *Instructions for the Cultivating and Raising of Flax and Hemp, in a Better Manner than Generally Practised in Ireland,* one of the first agricultural manuals to appear in the New World. So he decided to issue a pirated edition of the Bible.

If he was to escape detection, and a fine and possible imprisonment, his Bible would have to be similar in every respect to an English Bible. Henchman solved this problem by importing the type, the paper, and even the ink from England. Once he had the materials in hand, the production of the Bible moved ahead smoothly, and when the finished Bible appeared (issued under a false imprint so that the authorities would not suspect its true origin), it took a keen eye to detect any difference from a proper English Bible. Ironically, it was this clandestine operation that brought Henchman his greatest fame.

Intrigued as he was by the perilous adventures of his uncle and Daniel Henchman, John Hancock was more concerned at this point with a hazardous venture of his own: entrance examinations for Harvard College.

At thirteen, John was about to finish his instruction under Master Lovell at the South Grammar School, and the handful of boys planning to go on to college were already whispering among themselves about the terrors of Harvard examinations, held every year early in June. John knew that he would have to make a good showing. Uncle Thomas would expect it, and so would his grandfather, the Bishop of Lexington. His mother would be less concerned. She had remarried, and her attention was centered upon her new husband, the Reverend Daniel Perkins of Bridgewater. Reverend Perkins had children of his own, and Mary and Eben seemed to have become members of the Perkins clan. As the years passed, John saw increasingly less of his mother and Mary. Eben, however, was brought in to Boston for visits with his uncle and aunt; Thomas Hancock believed in keeping his eye on his male kin.

Before setting out for Cambridge, John knew by heart what form the examination would take. There would be a formal presentation to the President of Harvard and the four tutors. Then he would be taken aside by two of the tutors and quizzed relentlessly. Finally, he would be interviewed by the President. If he survived all these examinations, he would then be assigned an essay to write at home and given the college rules to copy out.

He went alone to Cambridge, by horseback and ferry. It had been difficult to dissuade Uncle Thomas from sending him in the carriage by way of "The Neck," but John knew it would be unwise to arrive with too much pomp. The candidate was supposed to be humble.

With Uncle Thomas and Aunt Lydia he had been to the village of Cambridge before, to attend the commencement festivities held each year in July. Even though Thomas Hancock had not attended Harvard, he gave the school all the support of an alumnus, and rumor was current that he would remember the college in his will. Perhaps the legacy would be cash, perhaps land, for the Hancock holdings were extensive. Even now, although the campus was small, the college owned orchards and fields stretching along the Charles River, acreage willed it by grateful graduates. Harvard was fond of Thomas Hancock, and it could be expected to show a certain fondness for his nephew.

John clenched the reins tighter as his horse approached the campus. The ordeal would soon be upon him. Here they were —Harvard Hall, Stoughton College and Massachusetts Hall, forming an open quadrangle around a court bare of trees except for one solitary elm. Slightly to the west of the quadrangle was the brick chapel.

Later, his memories of the quiz by the tutors were nothing

more than a blur, although he knew he had not distinguished himself. At South Grammar he had never been outstanding either as scholar or as dunce. Uncle Thomas had made it clear that the Hancock countinghouse did not need a Latin or Greek scholar; it needed a hard-headed man with a practical knowledge of business. And John's immediate future after college lay in the Hancock countinghouse. Where he might rise from there remained to be seen.

With the quiz over, John felt that the interview with President Holyoke went well. Holyoke had been a guest at the Hancock mansion, and John was at ease with him, despite the man's terrifying reputation as a stern disciplinarian. In any event, by the time John set out on his homeward journey, he knew that in mid-August he would be taking the route back to Cambridge for the start of classes.

When the college year began, John came equipped with the necessary knife, fork, mug, candles, and a lock for each of the chests holding his splendid wardrobe. His wardrobe was about the only taste of luxury he had; the routine at Harvard would have made a Spartan proud.

The students lived either in Massachuetts Hall or Stoughton Hall, sharing oak-paneled chambers with a roommate. Each class was assigned one of the four tutors, and not until their sophomore year did they encounter the two professors who comprised the remainder of the Harvard faculty.

Shy, witty, and slightly deaf, Edward Wigglesworth was the Professor of Divinity. But it was John Winthrop, Professor of Mathematics and Natural Philosophy for more than a decade, who inspired John Hancock with the most awe. Now thirty-six, a lean man of medium height, curious, orderly, he was a close friend of Benjamin Franklin and, next to Franklin, the greatest American scientist of his era. Winthrop had his lecture hall and laboratory on the second floor of Harvard Hall, and here he taught geometry, algebra, trigonometry, astronomy, geography, and such other science as was then known. For some of his students, "each new lecture seemed a new revelation." Others found the twists and turns of his mind much too difficult to follow. And Winthrop had his share of eccentricities, among them his periodic attempts to climb to the eaves of Stoughton College to measure the threatening bulge of the walls.

Most of the burden of actual instruction fell upon the tutors. The most famous of these was Henry Flynt, nicknamed "Father" by generations of students. When John Hancock came to Harvard in 1750, Father Flynt was seventy-five years old, and he had been a tutor for more than half a century. Short and thick-set, blind in one eye, as quick-tempered as he was warm-hearted, he was a learned man, a man who loved his charges.

During most of the year John struggled out of bed before the sun was up. At six o'clock, eyes still heavy with sleep, he stumbled over to morning prayers at the chapel, where the older boys took turns in reading from the Scriptures. Then came breakfast. The college steward was supposed to offer chocolate, tea, coffee and milk, with bread, biscuits and butter. But often, as John soon learned, there was only milk for his mug, and no butter for the bread or biscuits tossed on his pewter platter. Rather than waiting to eat in the dining hall, John usually ran back to the dormitory with his breakfast. If he bolted the meal fast enough, he could snatch a few minutes' extra sleep.

At eight o'clock he had to attend a lecture, then spend the remainder of the morning studying and reciting. For noon dinner he usually was offered boiled or roast mutton or beef with a slab of bread. After washing this down with a mug of cider, he dashed off for an afternoon of recitation and study. Evening prayers were held at five; he risked a heavy fine for being absent or tardy.

Supper, often meat pie with bread and milk, and a dessert of apple or cranberry pie, came at seven-thirty. On Saturdays, for a treat, there was salt fish, and sometimes a flour and water pudding boiled so hard it would bend a spoon. Food, rarely good, was often so bad it set off riots in the dining hall. John, with a full purse, could supplement these meager rations by outside purchases, but the poorer students, especially those paying their way by waiting on tables, were not so fortunate.

After supper John was free until nine o'clock, when a bell summoned him and his classmates to their chambers. This arduous schedule was broken by vacations twice a year. Summer vacation lasted six weeks, and a winter vacation of five weeks started the first Wednesday in January.

The curriculum, John discovered, was as rigorous as the diet. As a freshman he studied Greek, Latin, logic, rhetoric and physics. New subjects were added each year: natural philosophy for sophomores; moral philosophy, metaphysics and geography for juniors; mathematics and geometry for seniors. One day each week was devoted to theology, with an intensive study of the Bible. Although Harvard had grown to be more than a divinity school, many of the students still were preparing for the ministry.

John was glad that a student's rank in his class was determined by social position, not scholastic achievement. As the nephew of Boston's merchant prince, he found himself listed just below Samuel Quincy, son of Colonel Josiah Quincy of the Braintree Quincys, of whom he had stood in such awe as a boy. Sam's father had bought the Hancock parsonage and turned it into one of the social centers of Braintree life. (Years later, a sportsman to the end, Colonel Quincy was to die of a cold caught while sitting on a block of ice waiting to shoot ducks.)

A year older than John, Sam Quincy was brilliant, handsome, and devil-may-care, with a sophistication far beyond his years. He and John became close friends—and partners in dozens of escapades that made the college authorities fervently hope that Tutor Flynt was right when he insisted that "Wild colts often make good horses."

The college laws were strict, and fines were heavy, but John and Sam found these no obstacles. Harvard offered countless opportunities to indulge high spirits. The records of fines imposed on students reveal that the most popular misdeeds were card playing, profanity, lying, throwing stones through the tutors' windows, breaking open the doors of other students' rooms, making "tumultuous noises," "defiling the uninhabited parts of the College," "drinking prohibited liquors," burning fences on Guy Fawkes' Eve, skating on the Charles River without permission, and stealing geese and turkeys from Cambridge Common to roast at the fireplaces in the dormitories. Any student caught behaving frivolously on the Sabbath might be fined ten shillings. Although there were slightly less than a hundred students at Harvard, they made trouble out of all proportion to their number.

On one occasion in particular, Masters Hancock and Quincy found themselves in serious trouble. They were "degraded" several positions in their class for "being most remarkably active in making drunk" a local domestic "to Such a Degree as greatly indanger'd his Life."

A class behind Hancock—although a year older—was his childhood schoolmate from Braintree, John Adams. The bond between the two was never very close. Even this early in life the contrast in their characters was strong. Adams was serious, scholarly, and frugal, bluntly expressing his opinions, a perfectionist who was hard on himself and hard on any flaws he detected in his companions. Hancock had all the money he needed, and he spent it freely, on others as generously as upon himself. He worked hard enough when the occasion—or Uncle Thomas—demanded, but he was not a scholar by temperament.

His warmth and charm won friends easily, and he was eager, almost too eager, to be well liked. What undoubtedly irked Adams more than anything else, with his plain ways and plain tongue, was Hancock's swashbuckling manner. If Adams was essentially a Puritan, Hancock was at heart a Cavalier.

The months and years passed swiftly. In 1752 an epidemic of smallpox broke out in Boston, killing upwards of five hundred people. Eventually it made its way across the Charles River to Cambridge, causing the college to shut down in May for an extended summer vacation. In December John's grandfather, the Bishop of Lexington, died shortly before his eighty-second birthday. The next year the boys were saddened by the death of Professor Winthrop's young and popular wife. But, for the most part, John and his classmates were untroubled, continuing their studies—and pranks—as loyal subjects of King George II.

For all his good fortune as the favorite nephew of one of Boston's wealthiest merchants, John had never completely overcome the sense of loss at having been separated from his mother, sister, and brother. It seemed to John that Mary and Ebenezer had remained close to their mother, but that he had become the stranger, the outsider. When he heard a report in the spring of 1754 that Mary was betrothed, he reacted with a tinge of bitterness. "I should be Glad to know to whom," he wrote her. "I hope you will give me an Invitation, (whether the report be true or false I cannot tell.)" The report was true. Mary's fiancé was Richard Perkins, the son of their stepfather.

John soon forgot his irritation with Mary. July—and Commencement—were approaching, and his thoughts turned to the future. The years at Harvard had sped by. He had acquitted himself honorably enough as a student, although he was the first to admit that Sam Quincy, for one, had a more nimble wit, or that John Adams, for another, had a stronger passion for ideas.

Now he was impatient to try his hand as a man of business. The possibility that he might rise to a partnership in Thomas Hancock's far-flung enterprises seemed a glorious opportunity, and the sooner he set about rising, the better his chances would be. He was not without rivals for the favors of the great merchant. Uncle Thomas was keeping an eye on Eben and had promised to pay his way through Harvard. And John's aunt, Lucy Hancock Bowes, had a parcel of offspring clamoring for the attention of their wealthy uncle. At seventeen, John was canny enough to realize that if his future was to be sunny, he would have to work hard for his spot in the sun.

The Harvard Commencement, as one spectator observed, was "by far the most glorious Show in America." Nearly a month of preparations led up to the festivities on the second Wednesday in July. From near and far, relatives, friends, government officials, farmers, hired hands, peddlers, acrobats, entertainers, thieves and pickpockets poured into town. They came by ferry, in coaches, on horseback, and on foot, and some of them stayed on to celebrate for an entire week. Cambridge Common was covered with tents, booths, and a great horde of men, women, and children, all abandoning themselves to riotous merriment. This was the one time during the year that the Puritan community allowed itself free rein.

The arrival of the Hancock coach, groaning beneath the weight of Uncle Thomas and Aunt Lydia, drew an admiring crowd. No one, it was said, not even the Governor, had a more princely vehicle. John's mother and the Reverend Mr. Perkins drove in from Bridgewater, bringing Eben, Mary, and her fiancé, Richard Perkins. Even old Mrs. Hancock braved the dusty roads from Lexington to Cambridge to see her grandson graduate.

The actual Commencement ceremony began with a majestic procession to the meetinghouse—the undergraduates, the candidates for Master's degrees, the faculty, President Holyoke,

Governor Shirley and the members of His Excellency's Council. In the meetinghouse a platform had been erected around
the pulpit, and on it sat the dignitaries, splendid in ermine,
velvet, and silk, or in red-and-gold uniforms. Those in the seats
on the main floor wore costumes just as colorful: coats of
peach or lavender, waistcoats of embroidered satin laced with
gold, breeches and silk stockings of every hue, shoes glittering
with gold or silver buckles.

During the invocation by President Holyoke and the brief
sermon that followed, John kept stealing glances at the dazzling spectacle on the stage. It seemed to him that the mother
country herself could not offer a group of notables more imposing in dress and demeanor. With good fortune, he thought,
he himself might some day be sitting there in splendor as one
of the dignitaries of Massachusetts Bay.

Some four hours later the Latin orations by the outstanding
scholars were over, and so was the closing oration, delivered
in English. John and his fellow graduates were impatient for
the exercises to close, in order to be off to the dormitories,
where they had planned a lavish banquet for their families
and friends. It was the best way they knew to wipe away all
memory of the sorry fare they had eaten for four years in the
college dining hall.

Through all the celebrations, glittering with every bit of
magnificence that London could supply, paraded portly Uncle
Thomas and plump Aunt Lydia, beaming with joy at their
nephew. John could not escape the feeling that they felt more
pride in him than his own mother did. And, toward dark,
when he climbed into the great coach for the journey back to
Beacon Hill, he felt that he was truly going home.

IV

☆ ☆ ☆
☆

Apprentice Extraordinary

The years of peace and the business depression that so thoroughly depressed Thomas Hancock were drawing to an end. From the wilderness of the Ohio Valley word drifted back to Boston that soldiers under a young officer in the Virginia militia, George Washington by name, had been defeated at Fort Necessity by the French. It took little foresight to predict that France and England would soon be at war again.

Never one to be caught napping, Hancock began to cut down trade with any foreign ports that might be embroiled in hostilities, and he rerouted his vessels to the shipping lanes safest from enemy attack. Then he made ready to fill the lucrative government contracts certain to be his when war broke out.

Long a member of the Governor's Council, Merchant Hancock would soon be appointed His Majesty's Agent for Transports. His new position would give him the authority to pass out bounties to seamen who enlisted in His Majesty's service, to supply provisions to the vessels of the royal fleet, to hire freighters, issue sailing orders, and discharge crews back from a voyage. All this kept him busier than ever, and when he calculated the profits that rolled in from these duties as His Majesty's Agent, his loyalty to King George II increased in fervor.

After graduation, John was not allowed to loll about in the mansion on Beacon Hill. Instead, he was set to work in the main store, and even though he was not formally apprenticed to his uncle, for the next seven years he worked as hard as any young apprentice in Boston. Thomas Hancock treated his nephew well, but he expected—and got—full value for favors received.

For John, at seventeen, the store was a place of never-ending excitement. The headquarters of Uncle Thomas's far-flung operations was in the heart of town, within sight of Long Wharf and close to Dock Square with Faneuil Hall and its market. Just a block or so distant was the Town House, where the Council and House of Representatives met.

At one o'clock on working days, Boston merchants shut up their stores and warehouses and strolled over to the Town House. A covered walk on the ground floor functioned as an exchange where the merchants met their friends and rivals to discuss the day's business. Trying hard to assume a jauntiness and self-assurance he did not feel, John was often permitted to stroll along beside his uncle, shortening his long stride to match the portly merchant's step.

If Thomas Hancock was about to embark on a particularly hazardous scheme, he looked about the exchange for a partner to help provide capital and skill. These partnerships, John noticed, usually lasted no longer than the venture which called them into being. Uncle Thomas was delighted to share risks, but he did not enjoy sharing profits.

No session at the Town House was complete without a discussion of the latest dispatches from the other colonies and from England. The alert, bold-eyed young man soon made himself a favorite among the merchants; he was as eager to listen as they were to talk. By four o'clock John was back at the countinghouse, mulling over the transactions he had witnessed and the news he had heard of the outside world.

John soon discovered that business in the Hancock store was largely seasonal. Spring was hectic, and so was fall, but summer and winter were slack. The shelves of the store were filled with an astounding variety of merchandise, practically anything a customer could ask for. There were ribbons, cloth, and buckles; fans and swords; coal and lime, compasses, hour glasses, and larding pins; books and stationery; leather, salt, tea, and other provisions; and, if Aunt Lydia's own tastes indicate what the other gentlewomen of Boston required, countless bottles of double distilled lavender water.

This was merely the retail business. John was also busy with the wholesale operations: the provisioning of ships, the supplies for the garrisons in Nova Scotia, and the thousand and one details involved in supervising the loading and unloading of ships and the ordering of new merchandise. John realized, as never before, that buying and selling were but a small part of his uncle's activities. At times Thomas Hancock served as an agent for London merchants. He became entangled in such unrewarding tasks as ransoming prisoners and settling estates. He served as a banker and as a landlord. And he had to act as his own advertising manager and publicity agent, preparing handbills or inserting press notices when new shipments of goods arrived.

This large commercial business demanded considerable correspondence, and John was often required to lend a hand with the clerks. They had no typewriters and no carbon paper. Not only were all letters handwritten, but the file copies were laboriously transcribed into large letterbooks kept in the office. Mail was incredibly slow in reaching its destination, even intercolonial mail carried by the swiftest post riders. Letters to the mother country were frequently delayed for several weeks while a ship waited for sufficient cargo to fill her hold. With important letters, Thomas Hancock would order several copies made, to be deposited aboard different ships. There was no telling when a ship would be lost in a storm at sea, or captured by the enemy or pirates.

John threw himself into the work vigorously. Although all Boston took it for granted that he was Merchant Hancock's favorite and would become his heir, John knew that his uncle was too shrewd a businessman to turn over his empire to anyone he considered idle, slipshod, or inept. And there were rivals vying for his uncle's notice. Cousin Nicholas Bowes was now living with Daniel Henchman, Aunt Lydia's father. Cousin William Bowes had recently been introduced to Boston business circles by Uncle Thomas, who, before long, would be setting him up in the hardware business. John's position may have been enviable, but it was not yet secure.

Yet the work was so fascinating that he had few opportunities to fret about the competition for Uncle Thomas's attention. The store kept him busier than he had ever been at school, and as a storekeeper he proved more distinguished than as a scholar. "What a school this was!," observed his friend from Braintree, John Adams, now a senior at Harvard. "Four large ships constantly plying between Boston and London, and other business in proportion." John Hancock was "an example to all the young men of the town. Wholly devoted to business, he was as regular and punctual at his store as the sun in his course."

If John was an example to the young men of Boston, he was something more interesting to the young ladies. Nearly six feet tall and sturdily built, he had the manner and bearing of an aristocrat, and dashing good looks as well. His dark eyes were penetrating, his mouth was firm, his chin determined. With a fashionable wig covering his dark brown hair, wearing a coat of blue broadcloth laced with gold, a white waistcoat, and breeches of red velvet, he cut a handsome figure, from his three-cornered hat to his shoes with their glittering silver buckles. Aunt Lydia was quick to realize that her nephew was regarded as a prize catch, and she was constantly on the alert to keep him from taking the bait.

Early in 1755, soon after John's eighteenth birthday, a violent rainstorm from the southeast hurled itself upon the town. The large cranes on Long Wharf were broken down by the gale winds, and a high tide swept over the waterfront, damaging the shipping and the wharves. It was an ill omen, the superstitious said; greater disaster was on the way. The Hancocks, uncle and nephew, were thankful that their property on Long Wharf and Clark's Wharf suffered no great injury, but they were too busy to be concerned about prophecies of future catastrophe.

In the spring the British started preparing for an attack on Fort Beauséjour, the French post commanding the isthmus between Nova Scotia and Canada, and the Hancocks were commissioned to provision the force. For months they industriously lined up transports and gathered together food and military equipment.

By early June the expedition had reached Fort Beauséjour and forced it to capitulate. Now the British were faced with a dilemma. The Acadians, French colonists who had dwelled in Nova Scotia under British authority for more than forty years, posed a threat. The English feared that the Acadians were inciting the Indians and that they would rush to support an attack from French-held Louisbourg.

The only solution that the British saw was to expel these French colonists from Nova Scotia. After the harvest was over, the Acadians were persuaded to assemble at their parish churches, where they were suddenly surrounded by troops and heard their doom pronounced. Land, crops, cattle were de-

clared forfeit to the Crown. Their homes and barns were to
be burned. Men, women, and children were to be scattered
among the American colonies. At the point of bayonets more
than 6,000 of these unfortunates were herded aboard transports—transports furnished by Charles Apthorp, Boston merchant, and his partner, Thomas Hancock.

To Hancock, this was simply a business arrangement, and
he prided himself on being hard-headed and hard-hearted
about business matters. But when he came face to face with the
Acadians deposited in Boston, he suffered twinges from conscience as well as twinges from gout. To remedy matters, he
decided to convince the Governor's Council that the Acadians
should be allowed to remain as free settlers. The Council
agreed without much argument, for Thomas Hancock was
not the only Bostonian troubled by remorse.

A week or so after the Acadians arrived, Boston was struck
by the most dreadful earthquake it had ever experienced. The
tremors began about four o'clock in the morning and lasted
nearly five minutes. It seemed like an eternity. Trembling in
their beds, Uncle Thomas and Aunt Lydia expected "that the
house would sink or fall to pieces in a moment." When it was
all over Thomas noted with relief, "I had no hurt done to my
house or anything in it."

The next morning, when Merchant Hancock and his
nephew set out for the store in their carriage, they found the
cobblestone streets littered with debris. Hundreds of chim-
neys had been shattered; buildings had collapsed. All over
town clocks had stopped, and the weather van: on the Market
House had been thrown to the ground. But the Hancock store
was unharmed; the Hancock luck was holding.

During the next three years this good fortune continued.
Although trade in Boston came almost to a standstill and many
merchants suffered heavy losses, the two Hancocks bustled
about, seeing that government contracts were filled.

The British troops they supplied were not so fortunate. In skirmish after skirmish the soldiers of King George II suffered setbacks from French forces under the courtly Marquis de Montcalm. Not until Generals Amherst and Wolfe led the redcoats to victory at Louisbourg in July, 1758, did the British achieve a significant triumph.

In mid-September one of these conquering generals, Jeffrey Amherst, sailed into Boston Harbor aboard the 74-gun *Captain*. John Hancock stood just as much in awe as the rest of Boston at the display of British might that accompanied Amherst. Long Wharf, Clark's Wharf, Griffin's Wharf, and all the docks along the waterfront were crowded with British shipping. The men-of-war and transports from London and Louisbourg were an imposing sight. Nearly 5,000 soldiers disembarked and marched in a blaze of sound and color through the narrow, twisting streets to the green acres of the Common, where they set up camp. For the next few days, every time the Hancocks looked out from one of the front windows in the Beacon Hill mansion, the scarlet uniforms reminded them of the power of King George II. It was clear that the French and the Marquis de Montcalm would have to look to their laurels.

In the following year, 1759, France lost not only her laurels. She lost Fort Niagara, Crown Point, and finally Quebec. The fate of Canada—and of French power in North America—had been sealed. The French and Indian Wars were at an end. The New Englanders, almost as one man, breathed a sigh of relief. The threat of an alien neighbor in Canada and in the Ohio Valley had been removed, and with its removal the colonies began to feel themselves less dependent upon England for protection.

To Bostonians in the Hancocks' social circle, however, England was still "home," even though most of them had never been there. John Hancock, at twenty-three, was to be more favored. For six years he had labored zealously at the store, and Uncle Thomas now proposed to round out his training with a trip to England, a rare opportunity for a young colonial. It was not to be a mere sightseeing tour. If Thomas Hancock was to lay out £150 sterling for the passage, his nephew was expected to devote most of his time to business affairs and business contacts.

John felt that the trip held both a promise and a threat. If he did well, his reward on returning to Boston would be a partnership in the business: Thomas Hancock would become Thomas Hancock and Company. If he did not do well—that was left unsaid. Yet he had never been allowed to forget that his cousins, William and Nicholas Bowes, stood ready to step in if he should stumble; and now his brother, Eben, having gone through Harvard at Uncle Thomas's expense, was to come to work in the store. John had first claim upon his uncle's affections, but it was by no means the final claim.

Passage had been booked on a ship sailing early in the summer of 1760, but in February John's grandmother died in the parsonage at Lexington. Thomas Hancock, saddened by his mother's death, now hesitated to let his favorite nephew embark on a voyage that would keep him away from home for months on end. C644651 CO. SCHOOLS

From John's easy smile as he moved about his duties at the countinghouse, no one guessed how anxious he was. For months his thoughts had been turned toward England and toward London, which seemed to him the center of the fashionable world. He had been almost delirious with joy at the thought of setting out from home for the wide world—and of setting out as his own master. In his mind's eye he had already seen the London streets, the shops, the playhouses, the taverns, and the London ladies he planned to conquer with his bold charm and lively spirits. Such conquests, he thought, should prove easier than in Boston, where Aunt Lydia constantly outmaneuvered designing females and his own designs as well. Now his travels—and all the elegant amusements he had anticipated—were in jeopardy.

But as time passed, so did Uncle Thomas's reluctance to bid a temporary farewell to young Hancock. At last John was promised that when the *Benjamin & Samuel* had a full cargo and was ready to sail, he would be aboard. His heart bounded with joy, and he gave a cheer so loud it startled him as much as it did his majestic uncle.

V

A Colonial Abroad

In June, 1760, a crowd of well-wishers came down to Long
Wharf to see John Hancock off. Uncle Thomas and Aunt
Lydia were there, of course, together with their retinue of
servants and slaves—Hannah, Betsy, Molly, Cato, Agnes,
Prince, Scipio, and Hannibal. And because Thomas Pownall—
who had succeeded William Shirley as Royal Governor in
1757—was also sailing on the *Benjamin & Samuel*, the scene at
the dock assumed the proportions of a state occasion. As the
ship moved slowly out into Boston Harbor, Hannibal, John
noted, was "the last of the Family I Saw on the Wharff."

The voyage lasted nearly six weeks, but the companionship
of thirty-eight-year-old Pownall kept the younger man's spirits
high during the journey. Short, stout, and cheerful, Pownall
was returning to England for a visit before assuming new
duties. His good humor was unfailing. A favorite story among
Bostonians concerned his introduction to a matron several
inches taller than he was. In those days it was customary for
a gentleman to kiss a lady when presented to her. Governor
Pownall requested the towering matron to bend down.

"Never!" she replied. "I shall never stoop to any man—not
even to your Excellency."

With that, Pownall grabbed a nearby chair, hopped upon
it, and exclaimed, "Then I will stoop to you, madam!"

And, leaning over, he kissed her loudly upon the cheek.

In his three years as Governor of Massachusetts, Pownall
had achieved widespread popularity. Before he left, the Boston
town meeting voted him the honor of an "Address of Ack-
nowledgement," delivered by Thomas Hancock and a dozen
other prominent citizens. On the forty-day voyage across the
Atlantic Pownall proved a good friend to his young companion. In the hectic years that lay ahead he was to prove an
even better friend to the American colonies.

It was mid-July before Hancock reached England. London,
teeming with 750,000 human beings, was a dramatic contrast
to Boston, with its population of less than 20,000. This was
the London of brilliant actors, artists, and writers—David Gar-
rick, Sir Joshua Reynolds, Oliver Goldsmith, Dr. Samuel
Johnson. It was a city of fashionable mansions and stately
parks—St. James, Hyde Park, and Kensington Gardens with its
Broad Walk, Round Pond, and Serpentine, so impressive that
Boston Common seemed a mere cow pasture by comparison.

It was also a city in which thugs, thieves, and pickpockets
roamed even the most fashionable thoroughfares in broad daylight as well as in the dark of night.

The crowded streets, their cobbles slippery with mud and
sewage, cluttered with carriages, were alive with a bustle and
business the likes of which young Hancock had never seen in
Boston. The noise, the swarm of people, the glare of shops and
signs filled him with a constant excitement.

And the Thames! John thought back to the Boston waterfront with its crowded wharves, but in no way could it com-
pare with the Thames River as a great channel of trade. One
day, sailing on the river, John estimated that he had seen more

than 1,400 ships at anchor between the Tower of London and Limehouse.

No place in the world, it was said, could a man live more to his own mind—or whim—than in London. Uncle Thomas was aware of the temptations, and John soon received a letter of warning. "Write me how the World goes on that Side of the Water," he asked. "Be frugal of Expences, do Honor to your Country & furnish Your Mind with all wise Improvements." And, he added, "Keep the Pickpockets from my Watch."

While in London John stayed at the home of his uncle's friend and associate, merchant Jonathan Barnard, and Barnard's shop in Size Lane became Hancock's business headquarters. Barnard took an immediate liking to the mannerly young colonial and helped him to make important business contacts. Full of ambition, John was determined to show that Uncle Thomas's trust in him was not misplaced. His new business acquaintances found him deferential, but a firm and capable negotiator.

Each Sunday the Barnards made it a point to take John to hear the sermon at a different church, and London abounded with them—St. James's, St. George's, St. Margaret's, St. Martin's, St. John's, St. Mary le Strand, St. Clement's, St. Dunstan's, St. Bride's. John was quite overwhelmed by their magnificence.

His hosts also made sure that he visited the House of Lords soon after his arrival. There the young merchant from Boston saw George II, King of Great Britain, sitting on his throne. It was a sight Hancock thought he would treasure in his memory forever.

Governor Pownall provided him with an entrée to society. Although Hancock was a little awed at first, his vivacity, his love of fun, his obvious pleasure in good company made him welcome everywhere. His entertainment was not confined to the stately homes of his new acquaintances. Before long, he was a familiar figure at the theatres, pleasure gardens, and coffeehouses.

Out of sight of Aunt Lydia's piercing eyes, John was inclined to run up and down town like a wild colt. London society, high or low, seemed abloom with beautiful young girls, and John found them as susceptible to his charms as he was to theirs, from the fine aristocratic lasses to the pretty little servant maids.

All these flirtations involved considerable expenses, not the least of which was his tailor's bill. A fashionable beau was forced to maintain an elaborate wardrobe, which might contain such items as a pink suit with gold buttons, a coat and trousers of bluish green, black velvet breeches, a waistcoat of white satin laced with gold, a long scarlet coat reaching below the knee, cambric ruffled shirts, and, of course, a multitude of wigs and cocked hats.

This extravagance was a bit difficult to justify to Uncle Thomas. "To Appear in Character," he wrote, "I am Obliged to be pretty Expensive. I find Money some way or other goes very fast, but I think I can Reflect it has been spent with Satisfaction and to my own honour." Then, in honesty, he was forced to add, "I fear if you was to see my Tailor's Bill, you would Think I was not a very plain Dressing person."

Just as John was getting into step as a young man of fashion, an event of singular importance took place. On Saturday morning, October 25, 1760, in the palace at Kensington, King George II, after rising as usual, complained of not feeling well, fell down in a fit of apoplexy, and died on the spot.

Like his fellow Bostonians, John Hancock had considered George II a passably good king and was curious what manner of ruler his grandson and heir would prove to be. The twenty-two-year-old heir apparent was proclaimed King George III on Sunday, the day following his grandfather's death. Throughout all London, John wrote home, there was "great

Pomp and Joy." The coronation, scheduled for April, was an event John looked forward to eagerly. It would be, he thought, "the grandest thing I shall ever meet with."

The pomp and joy John wrote about soon gave way to a period of traditional national mourning. The theatres closed, and there were no public diversions. Even private entertaining was kept to a minimum. John complained that "Every thing here now is very dull." But soon he was busy getting himself the proper mourning to wear, and, so rumor had it, he was carrying on a new flirtation with a saucy young servant girl.

A letter from Ebenezer Hancock brought news of their sister Mary's wedding to Richard Perkins. John was quick to congratulate her and to compliment Eben on his progress in Uncle Thomas's store. On his return to Boston, John said, he expected to find Eben "a complete merchant," advising him to "give great attention to business and let your conduct be such as to merit the Esteem of all about you." In another letter he told Eben, "By all means study to please your Uncle and Aunt, to whom you are bound by all the Ties of Gratitude and Love."

At the moment, Uncle Thomas and Aunt Lydia were not completely happy with John's behavior. They complained that he was not writing frequently enough, that he was being a spendthrift, that he was staying away from home too long. John hastened to explain that he had written many letters; perhaps the ships carrying them had been captured or disappeared at sea. As for being a spendthrift, John was hard put to offer a plausible defense.

One of John's main reasons for remaining in London was his eagerness to attend the Coronation. It was certain to be a grand and splendid ceremony, and his heart leapt at the prospect of the pomp and pageantry. George III, he noted, was "very popular and much Beloved."

Tradition has it that the handsome young Bostonian was

presented at Court, where the King honored him with the
gift of a gold snuffbox bearing a likeness of His Royal High-
ness. If John did receive such a memento, he surely guarded it
even more carefully than his uncle's watch from the prying
hands of London's pickpockets. On his return to Boston it
would be something to show with pride to the colonial gentlemen—and ladies. Moreover, he might hope that, in years to
come, His Majesty would recollect their meeting if ever the
name of Hancock were being considered for a royal appointment.

The pace John set himself in London soon took its toll, and
he was confined to the house with illness. The Barnards took
good care of him, and he was tended devotedly by a young
woman who strongly reminded him of Hannah, one of Aunt
Lydia's servants. But, as he confessed in a letter home, if he had
to lie abed feeling so miserable, he wanted to be in his own
bed in the Beacon Hill mansion, with Hannah herself tending
to his needs.

Before long he was back on his feet and back in stride, seeing new sights, making new friends. But as the weeks length-
ened into months, he began to feel pangs of homesickness.
Letters from home would have helped, but not very many
arrived. Eight months passed before he received a single letter
from his mother or stepfather.

Early in March he wrote to the Reverend Perkins, "I shall
with satisfaction bid adieu to this grand place with all its
pleasurable enjoyments and tempting scenes, for the more
substantial pleasures which I promise myself in the enjoyment
of my friends in America." Yet the scenes in London were
tempting, and soon, in a letter to Eben, he admitted being torn
between an impulse to return home and his desire to stay on
for the Coronation, which had been delayed until a suitable
wife could be found for the King.

Back in Boston the Hancocks found the Beacon Hill mansion a lonely place without John. Eben was proving a disappointment in the store. He lacked John's flair for getting along with people, and at times Uncle Thomas came home convinced that the boy had no head for business. As for the Bowes brothers, Nicholas and William, they were hard workers, but their companionship was not as entertaining as John's, nor were they as attentive.

Then Aunt Lydia's father died, and her loneliness increased. Uncle Thomas wrote that she missed John sorely. "Indeed," he remarked, "I want you very much."

This amounted almost to a command to return to America. Coronation or no Coronation, John could not delay his departure much longer, so he turned his attention to buying presents for his homecoming, among them a cap and French horn for Cato. By July he was able to inform Uncle Thomas that he would be under way by the end of the month.

On the long voyage home aboard the *Boscawen*, John had many days and nights in which to look back on his experiences in England. He had done his work well—settled accounts favorably, gathered inside information about the Board of Ordnance, and established personal contacts that would stand the Hancock organization in good stead in the years to come. Surely Uncle Thomas would be pleased.

The year in England had brought John new understandings. King George III would never be merely a stiff figure in a portrait, or a shadowy monarch sitting on a shadowy throne. The King of Great Britain was a man Hancock had seen in the flesh, a man a year younger than himself.

John had been to the House of Lords and the House of Commons and listened to the debates. True, Parliament was a much more august assemblage than the Massachusetts General Court, but both groups were composed of human beings, capable—like all men—of good or evil, wisdom or folly.

The young traveler looked back on his year in England

with affection, admiration, and delight. No longer was the mother country just a misty, distant land across the wide Atlantic. Yet no longer would he view someone born in England with indiscriminate awe. London-born or Boston-born, the man was an Englishman, deserving similar privileges. And John came home convinced that it was his right, as an Englishman, to speak out against any abuse of these privileges.

VI

☆ ☆ ☆
☆

Heir to a Fortune

When John reached Massachusetts in early October, 1761, he found that tempers in Boston had begun to flare. First of all, Thomas Hutchinson, a member of one of Boston's oldest families, seemed about to garner a monopoly of political offices. Highly intelligent, with a toughness that belied his delicate features and soft hazel eyes, Hutchinson had already distinguished himself as a supporter of the King's policies whether or not these policies were in the best interests of the Province. When, early in 1761, Hutchinson was appointed Chief Justice of the Superior Court of Massachusetts, the appointment caused heated discussions in the coffeehouses about the town. Hutchinson already was Lieutenant Governor, Judge of Probate, and a member of the Governor's Council. Was there to be no end to his power?

And had not the office of Chief Justice—now granted to Hutchinson—been promised to the highly respected Colonel Otis, father of the brilliant young lawyer, James Otis? From this point on, young Otis was Hutchinson's bitter enemy. It was claimed James Otis had sworn revenge, "that he would set the province in flames, if he perished by the fire."

There was another reason for uneasiness. The wealthy Hutchinsons had intermarried with the wealthy Olivers. Thomas Hutchinson's brother-in-law, Peter Oliver, was also a Chief Justice. And another brother-in-law, Andrew Oliver, was Secretary of the Province. It was whispered, muttered, spoken aloud—too much power was being concentrated in the hands of too few.

Then the customs officials caused another tempest by attempting to enforce the Navigation Acts, regulating trade in the colonies. Although the Acts had been in existence for decades, the Boston merchants, bent on profits, had blithely ignored them. The controversy came to a head when the officers of the Crown applied for a renewal of the general writs of assistance, which had expired with the death of King George II. These general writs enabled customs officials to enter stores, warehouses, or homes to search for contraband goods; they amounted, in effect, to a general search warrant.

Sixty-three of the Boston merchants banded together to oppose renewal of the writs, hiring James Otis and Oxenbridge Thacher to present their case. When the case was heard, Thacher spoke first, presenting the merchants' side calmly, reasonably, dispassionately. Then came Otis, huge, rough, eagle-eyed, a man of dazzling and erratic genius. He spoke for hours with fiery eloquence, electrifying his audience as he denounced the writs as being against the fundamental principles of laws, against man's inalienable rights of liberty and property. Despite Otis's thrilling presentation, the merchants lost their case. Nevertheless, colonial opposition to the Crown had been strengthened.

Although Uncle Thomas was still in a rage about the writs when John returned home, he did too much business with the Crown to voice his disapproval too loudly. John was more impetuous. Within a year of his arrival back in Boston he had joined the Masonic Lodge of St. Andrew's, which numbered among its members such outspoken critics of Parliament as the twenty-six-year-old goldsmith and engraver, Paul Revere, and the eloquent Dr. Joseph Warren, just two years out of Harvard College. There is reason to suppose that John Hancock was one of the first to join the secret Long Room Club, so called because it met in the long room above the shop where the *Boston Gazette* was printed. Samuel Adams, James Otis, Joseph Warren, Paul Revere, and Dr. Benjamin Church were also probably among the members. No records were kept at the Long Room Club; the debates and discussions were too inflammatory.

Despite his promise to make John a partner, Thomas Hancock was in no hurry to take this important step. Perhaps he was worried about the crowd of men to whom his nephew seemed so strongly drawn; the radical political views of Sam Adams, James Otis, and Joseph Warren were highly distasteful to the conservative merchant.

Perhaps Merchant Hancock wished to test John further, to make doubly sure he warranted the high honor of partnership. After all, Nicholas and William Bowes were also his nephews, as was Eben Hancock, for all his limitations. But most likely Thomas Hancock was simply reluctant to relinquish any portion of his absolute authority.

In any event, it was not until January 1, 1763, as John was approaching his twenty-sixth birthday, that Thomas Hancock wrote to Jonathan Barnard in London: "I have this Day Taken my Nephew Mr. John Hancock, into Partnership with me, having had long Experience of his Uprightness, & great Abilities for Business." The firm, he points out, is henceforth to be known as Thomas Hancock & Company.

Merchant Hancock's decision to make his nephew a partner was given a final impetus by his own failing health. Gout and a nervous disorder were getting the better of him. During the three months after the start of the partnership, he was confined to his bed by illness, expecting "to be able to attend to very little Business again, if any."

Thus the whole weight of conducting the vast business was suddenly thrust upon John's shoulders. It was a heavy burden. Just before taking to his bed, Uncle Thomas had entered into an agreement with an Englishman named Matthew Woodford to supply two garrisons in Nova Scotia: Annapolis Royal and Chignecto. Even though the operation showed a profit, it provided more than the usual share of headaches.

"We have a very hard Winter & no Communication at present," Thomas Hancock complained, "with Annapolis or Chignecto, all froze up & no Navigation can Stir to or from thence." The firm was furnishing bread, pork, and other provisions, but it was unusually difficult to keep track of accounts because of the many changes of commanding officers and the "Deaths of Commissarys, one after another." By May the firm was attempting to lay in enough provisions to keep the posts supplied until Christmas, "Purchasing every thing at the Cheapest rates." Apparently some of these cheap provisions consisted of bad bread, for a few months later a letter to Matthew Woodford admitted that "Mr. Williams has got clear of all the old Bread except 1140 lb., but we were obliged to send him from Boston a Quantity of higher prized Bread for the officers, &c., to help it off & make 'em easy." The troops were "complaining of having so much Rice"; pork had risen to the fantastic price of fifteen dollars a barrel; bread and flour had to be ordered all the way from Philadelphia. Moreover, the firm was in a great rush to get provisions on the way because by October the seas would be too rough for sailing. There seemed no end to their troubles.

By now Thomas Hancock was hobbling about again, although he was no longer the man who could strike terror into the hearts of his competitors. Weak as he was physically, the spirit of battle was still strong, and he was determined to venture once more into the highly competitive whale oil market. A Nantucket firm was to do the buying; Thomas Hancock & Company would handle the shipping; and Jonathan Barnard's firm would market the oil in London.

For this reason the Hancocks decided to build a 160-ton vessel "solely for the London Trade," to be launched in September, 1763, and called the *Boston Packet.* They aimed to make her "a prime going Ship, handsome & to Carry well, plain but neat."

Both uncle and nephew used every wile at their command to corner the whale oil trade, and they had high expectations of success. Thomas wrote to London, boasting, "We would just observe to You that this Whale Oil, is far preferable to what commonly is at Your market, it is quite white & sweet, & well manufactured." His confidence that it would fetch a much better price than ordinary brown sperm proved correct.

Several of the Hancock vessels were able to cross the Atlantic with cargoes that brought extremely good prices, but the firm was not able to gain a complete monopoly. A schooner owned by one of their competitors managed to get away from Nantucket, despite some obvious skulduggery by one of the Hancocks' associates. "Capt. Folger did all he could to prevent her sailing," Thomas wrote, "but they were Determined upon it."

Merchant Hancock's health was growing increasingly worse. "I am very weak & cannot get well," he wrote. "My Legs & Feet swell much & I am Incapable of Doing hardly any Business." But he was not a man to give up easily.

Meanwhile, his nephew was seeking solace from business problems in the company of Sally Jackson, daughter of Joseph Jackson, one of the Boston selectmen. John had met her soon after returning from London, and her pert and pretty manner had captivated him. Even though Aunt Lydia did not approve of the young lady, John continued to court her for year after year, until he met an even prettier and more vivacious girl, who won Aunt Lydia's heart as well as his own. Perhaps it was to impress Miss Jackson that John asked his London agent to have made to order "1 neatt Bag wig and 1 neatt Bob wig. Fashionable & of a light colour."

In January, 1764, a terrible epidemic of smallpox was raging through Boston, distracting John from both romance and business. Warning flags were hung before the houses of at least twenty-five families, and there was a mass exodus to the country. Most of the merchants and traders carted their stock out of town and opened stores in private homes in the surrounding villages. The Governor, with his Council and the House of Representatives, fled to Cambridge, carrying on their duties in Harvard Hall and the newly built Hollis Hall. Thomas Hancock, as a member of the Council, went along, accompanied by Aunt Lydia and John. Even in Cambridge they were not safe from calamity, for Harvard Hall caught fire and burned to the ground in the midst of a snowstorm. President Holyoke's daughter reported that "Mr. Hancock, who lodged out on account of the storm, lost everything except the clothes he had on."

By July the Hancocks were back in Boston, planning another campaign to corner the whale oil market. This time they were victorious, dispatching both the *Boston Packet* and the brig *Lydia* before their main competitor, Rotch of Nantucket, could get a vessel under way. "Oil is extremely high and scarce which you will Notice in the Sale," Thomas wrote elatedly to London. "We have been so very Lucky in purchasing a Cargo of Oil, for this vessell & think we have Gained a Great Point, when Mr. Rotch's vessell lays waiting for Oil & she began to Load before Our Brig^t was Ready to Take & indeed while the Boston Packett was Load'g."

As master of the *Lydia* for this voyage the Hancocks had engaged a young man who was to figure importantly in the Hancock story, Captain James Scott. Thomas Hancock was very impressed by the man's ability, but he took the precaution of writing to his London agent, ". . . advice Mr. Scott against incurring any needless Expences on the Brig't, & pray Recommend Prudence & care to him, as he is Young, & let him advise with you, Respecting his conduct."

On the return voyage Thomas requested that the *Boston Packet* bring two items for his personal use: ten gross of the best quart champagne bottles, and an eiderdown covering, which would make him more comfortable as he lay ill in bed with the gout.

The eiderdown covering arrived, but not in time for Thomas Hancock to make use of it. On the first day of August, just about noon, he drove down to the Town House to attend a meeting of the Council. As he was entering the chamber, he was stricken with apoplexy, and at three o'clock that afternoon he died. He was sixty-two years old.

His funeral, as grand a one as John and Aunt Lydia could arrange, was held on August 6. Thomas Hancock's escutcheon was hung above the doorway of the Beacon Hill mansion; the shutters were closed; the mirrors covered with white sheets. The funeral procession itself was an imposing cavalcade, headed by all the dignitaries of the town. The leading merchant of Boston went to his grave with all the pomp and ceremony with which he had lived.

The will contained an abundance of bequests. Harvard was to receive £1,000 toward the founding of a professorship of Oriental languages. The Society for Propagating the Gospel Among the Indians also was to get £1,000, and the Society for Carrying on the Linen Manufactory, £200. The town of Boston was left £600 to establish an insane asylum. If Cato behaved well, he was to receive his freedom on reaching thirty.

Among various legacies to relatives and friends, Ebenezer Hancock was allotted slightly less than £700 and some land along the Kennebec River.

Aunt Lydia was bequeathed £10,000, the Beacon Hill mansion and grounds and furnishings, the slaves, coaches, and carriages.

And John Hancock, Uncle Thomas's favorite nephew and partner, found himself heir to more than £70,000, a sum that made him, at twenty-seven, a millionaire in an era when millionaires were rare indeed.

VII

☆ ☆ ☆
☆

The Merchant Turns Politician

As the richest man in New England and probably the second richest man in all the colonies, John Hancock suddenly found himself a person of tremendous importance. He had been left his uncle's business, credit, capital, and fortune—and the protection of his uncle's widow. Aunt Lydia, however, seemed quite capable of protecting herself. With her protuberant, beetle-black eyes, stern eyebrows, firm lips, and wattles under a determined chin, she presented a picture of a dowager fearless and unassailable. A friend once described her as being "as ladylike a woman as Boston ever bred," a masterpiece of understatement. From the way Aunt Lydia was to manage John's love life, it looked as if she protected him as much as he protected her.

His sudden importance seems not to have shaken John Hancock from his usual course. Even his old acquaintance, lawyer John Adams, who could bring a waspish tongue to bear on anyone of whom he disapproved, was forced to admit, "No alteration appeared in Mr. Hancock. . . . The same steady, punctual, industrious, indefatigable man of business; and, to

53

complete his character with the ladies, always genteelly dressed, according to the fashions of the day."

Having seen the styles in London and possessing enough money to indulge any whim, John took care to dress in a blaze of colors and ruffles, a fashion so dazzling it often filled his less prosperous and more soberly costumed acquaintances with envy. But the young ladies of Boston (and their mothers) found him fascinating. Handsome, gallant, generous, and fabulously rich, he was by far the most eligible bachelor in Boston. Had Aunt Lydia not been hovering in the background, he could easily have been overwhelmed.

Even though John himself favored Miss Sally Jackson, she was having a difficult time in the face of Aunt Lydia's opposition, but her pretty charms managed to keep the courtship going for nearly ten years. Aunt Lydia, however, had her eye on another prospect, Dorothy Quincy. Dolly, only seventeen, lived in Braintree, and like all the Braintree Quincys had a mind and will of her own. Yet once Aunt Lydia had set her heart upon something, no earthly power could deter her, and she had set her heart on Dolly Quincy as the wife for John.

At the moment John Hancock was more concerned with his business responsibilities than with female hearts. "What shall I say of his fortune, his ships?" John Adams reminisced in later years, after both he and John Hancock had left their mark on American history. "His commerce was a great one . . . not less than a thousand families were, every day in the year, dependent upon Mr. Hancock for their daily bread. Consider his real estate in Boston, in the country, in Connecticut, and the rest of New England. Had Mr. Hancock fallen asleep to this day, he would now awake one of the richest men. Had he persevered in business as a private merchant, he might have erected a house of Medicis." Hancock did not fall asleep, and he did not persevere as a private merchant. Instead, within a few years, he threw his considerable energies and even more considerable fortune into the service of the people.

But now more business troubles were brewing. Just before Thomas Hancock's death, ships in from London brought word that Parliament had passed a new Sugar Act, to go into effect toward the end of September, 1764. Among other revenues, a duty of threepence was to be levied on molasses. What alarmed the colonists was not the size of the duty, but the fact that it was levied to raise revenue for the Crown rather than to regulate trade. Moreover, the traditional indulgence toward smuggling was at an end. The new duties were to be strictly enforced. Almost at once Sam Adams and James Otis began to raise the cry that taxation without representation was illegal and arbitrary.

Now almost forty-two, Samuel Adams had established himself as a failure in the eyes of most Bostonians. His father, a merchant and brewer, having lost a fortune in a scheme to circulate paper money, died a bankrupt. A Harvard education seemed to have taught Sam little. He was dismissed by his first employer for devoting more time to politics than to his duties. He allowed the remnants of his father's brewery business to slip through his fingers. With some friends he founded a newspaper, *The Independent Advertiser*, which soon ceased publication.

Even in politics his career, up to this point, had been notoriously undistinguished. In 1746 he had been elected one of the clerks of the Boston market, and in 1753 he was elected town scavenger. By 1764 he had been tax collector for Boston for eight years, but rumors were increasing that he was short in his accounts. Few people suspected him of dishonesty. Everyone knew he had no interest in keeping his books straight, nor could he bring himself to force the underprivileged to pay their taxes. His cousin, country lawyer John Adams, thirteen years his junior, had almost given up hope that Sam would ever amount to anything.

In the outcry against the Sugar Act, James Otis was the man who took the center of the stage. But behind the scenes Sam Adams was at work; his genius for politics and propaganda was beginning to mature. At the moment Sam was cultivating an acquaintance with John Hancock, who was being seen with increasing frequency at the meetings of the political clubs with which Boston abounded.

Hancock, however, had much on his mind besides politics. As best he could, John coped with the day-to-day trials of business in Boston. "I continue in the same store," he wrote to London, "and propose carrying on the same business as with my late Uncle, by myself." Eben, either in indignation at his small inheritance, or in a fit of ill-advised independence, had decided to leave the store and go into partnership with a man named Blanchard. John did what he could to help, writing to Barnard and other English merchants that he would back the new partners to the extent of £500.

Eben's departure from the store was actually a bit of good luck for his older brother. Soon after this, a young man of twenty-three named William Palfrey presented himself for employment. Scarcely of medium height, Palfrey made up for his lack of physical stature by an abundance of cheerfulness and good sense. It was a fortunate association for both men. Except for a brief interval, Palfrey served Hancock wisely and faithfully until the outbreak of the Revolution. In 1780 he was appointed consul-general to France, and at this point his luck ran out. The ship on which he sailed from America was never heard from again.

Almost as soon as John took over the Hancock business, Boston was struck by a severe depression. A prominent merchant named Wheelwright failed, and from that moment on firms collapsed like houses of cards. "I would advise you to be careful who you trust," Hancock wrote to his London associates; "times are very bad & precarious here & take my word, my good Friends, the times will be worse here, in short such is the situation of things here that we do not know who is and who not safe."

Nevertheless, he continued to pull in profits from supplying the Nova Scotia garrisons, and he made a trip to Nantucket to build up his contacts in the whale oil trade, once again entering into a fierce competition with William Rotch. "I can have what Oyl I please & of the best men there," he wrote on his return, "which of course, takes from the other Channell and is very chagrining to Mr. R——h but he knows my mind." The competition meant that John had to move fast at every opportunity. "I must either sell my vessels or keep them running," he stated; "it will not do for me to be idle and let others (and R——h) buy up."

Soon Rotch paid a visit to Boston, dropping by the Hancock store for a chat. Hancock, in turn, invited the Nantucket merchant to dinner in order to discuss a joint attempt to control the trade in oil. "I have had a long Conference with Mr. Rotch agreeable to your desire, Respecting oyl trade," he wrote to Barnard. "He appears to be upon amicable terms . . . You are not so well acquainted with that Gent as I am; but will for once try him."

John's scepticism about Rotch was well-founded. Within a month the arrangement had broken down, and it was each man for himself. However, his hopes of success were undiminished. "In the course of another year," he noted, "I shall be at a better certainty with respect to oyl having concerns in whaling vessels, with persons at Nantuckett and Martha's Vineyard, that with Common Success I may meet a large Supply out of my own vessels. I have now four vessels and believe another year shall increase ye number."

Late in March, 1765, Parliament passed a bill that was to

cause havoc in the colonies: the Stamp Act, scheduled to go into effect on November 1. Stamp duties were to be levied on almost every piece of paper used in any sort of business in the colonies: legal papers, wills, licenses, deeds, mortgages, leases, bills of lading, customs clearances, almanacs, newspapers, books, pamphlets, playing cards, and dice. It was the first direct tax ever levied by Parliament upon America, and the colonists feared it would be the first of many. Moreover, one of its main purposes was to raise revenue to support the military establishment in America, which, the colonists insisted, they did not want.

John Hancock became increasingly involved in the political storm that swept through Boston. In March, 1765, with the backing of James Otis and Sam Adams, he was elected one of the Boston selectmen at the town meeting. In the months and years that followed, the Boston town meeting was to raise a voice that grew steadily louder.

Rumors of the passage of the Stamp Act reached John in April. "I hear the stamp act is to take place," he wrote to Barnard in London; "it is very cruel, we were before much burthened, we shall not be able much longer to support trade, and in the end Great Britain must feel the ill effects of it. I wonder the merchants and friends to America don't make some stir for us."

Meanwhile, a secret organization known as the Sons of Liberty, was forming. Although Sam Adams was not one of the nine known original members, it was whispered about town that the group had its genesis at his suggestion. And it was also whispered that the Sons of Liberty were planning active resistance to the detested Stamp Act. The Sons of Liberty did their work well. Early on a Wednesday morning in mid-August, two effigies were discovered hanging from a huge elm—henceforth to be known as the Liberty Tree—at the junction of Essex and Newbury Streets. One figure represented a stamp officer; the other, the Devil. The stamp officers, colonials appointed by the Crown to distribute the hated stamps, were to be a special target for abuse.

Throughout the day a jeering crowd gathered around the elm tree. About dusk the figures were taken down, placed on a bier, and borne through the streets of the town, followed by a mob chanting, "Liberty and Property! No Stamps!" Governor Francis Bernard, who had succeeded Thomas Pownall back in 1760, was still in session with his Council at the Town House as the mob paraded by. From there the procession marched down to the waterfront and demolished a small building erected to serve as a Stamp Office. Then they swarmed up to the top of Fort Hill, where they roasted the effigies in a huge bonfire.

The mob was not yet finished. Their next target was the home of Andrew Oliver, Secretary of the Province and newly appointed Stamp Master. Armed with clubs and staves, they broke in, shouting their determination to stand up for their rights and liberties as Englishmen. The next morning Andrew Oliver resigned.

"I hope," John Hancock noted, "the same Spirit will prevail throughout the whole Continent."

Two nights later the mob was on the move again. This time their goal was the home of Oliver's brother-in-law, Lieutenant Governor Thomas Hutchinson. Warned of the mob's approach, Hutchinson refused to flee despite the pleas of his family, but he did have the doors and windows barred. Surrounding the splendid mansion, the crowd called out for Hutchinson to appear on his balcony to deny that he had written to England urging passage of the Stamp Act. Never a man to bow to the mob, he stood firm behind the closed doors. While the crowd was debating what to do, one of the neighbors called from a window. The Lieutenant Governor and his family, the neighbor said, had left for their country home earlier in the evening. The crowd muttered, then fell silent, and finally dispersed.

While Sam Adams was stirring up the Sons of Liberty, Hancock was writing to London merchants to urge them to bring pressure in Parliament for the repeal of the Stamp Act. "It is a Cruel hardship upon us & unless we are Redressd we must be Ruin'd," he said. "Do Exert yourselves for us and promote our Interest with the Body of Merchants the fatal Effects of these Grievances you will very Sensibly feel; our Trade must decay & indeed already is very indifferent."

On Monday evening, August 26, trouble was on foot again. About twilight a firewarden discovered a bonfire burning in King Street, a strange thing for a humid summer night. When he started to put it out, he was struck from behind and forced to flee.

Soon after this, whoops and whistles were heard. A crowd assembled at the house of Charles Paxton, Surveyor of Customs. The owner of the house, assuring them that Paxton had departed, offered a barrel of punch as consolation. After finishing the punch, the mob attacked the home and office of Justice Storey, destroying his private papers, court files, and account books.

By now the crowd seemed seized by lunacy. Whooping, roaring, jeering, they rushed on toward the new and elegantly furnished home of Benjamin Hallowell, Comptroller of Customs. Wholesale havoc resulted. They tore down the fence, broke the windows, smashed chairs, tables, glass, china, and everything else they could lay their hands on. By the time they had consumed all the stores in the wine cellar, they were in a blind and drunken rage.

Hutchinson's three-storied mansion was the next target. Breaking down the doors with axes, smashing the windows, a flood of men poured in. Hutchinson had been determined to face the ruffians, but his eldest daughter refused to go without him. They barely escaped in time.

Until daylight the vandals swarmed through the house, destroying or dumping in the street what they could not carry away. Every piece of clothing belonging to the family was ripped to shreds; furniture was hacked to splinters; the finest private library in New England—including the manuscript for the second volume of Hutchinson's *History of Massachusetts Bay*—was cast into the gutter. Not content with this, the mob tore the wainscotting from the walls, knocked down partitions, tried to pry bricks from the walls. They climbed to the roof, uprooted the cupola, sent it crashing down into the street. Finally they fell upon the wine cellar.

By dawn what had been one of the most handsome homes in the colonies was nothing but a shell from top to bottom. All Boston was shocked, outraged, even a little terrified by this display of mob violence. That morning the citizens of the town (including a number who had been among the mob) assembled in Faneuil Hall and by unanimous vote condemned the misdeeds of the night before. Sam Adams denounced the deeds as "high-handed outrages"; John Hancock declared that the injury done to Hutchinson is "what I abhor and detest as much as any man breathing."

In the lull that followed the Stamp Act riots a special town meeting was called to elect a member to the House of Representatives to replace lawyer Oxenbridge Thacher, who had died in July. Samuel Adams, John Rowe, John Huddock, and John Hancock were the candidates. Adams was elected; Hancock ran a poor fourth. Instead of being discouraged, he became increasingly active in the Liberty Party, as the group composed of Sam Adams, Otis, Warren, and Benjamin Church was coming to be known.

After Thomas Hancock's death, the acquaintance between John Hancock and Sam Adams had ripened into friendship.

They were, in many ways, an oddly matched pair. More than fourteen years older than Hancock, Sam Adams was now beginning to emerge as a figure of consequence. He was, however, perilously near being thrust in jail over the shortages in his tax accounts. Just in time Hancock came to his aid with a substantial loan.

Adams's dress still reflected a disregard for the practical things of life. His brown coat was shabby, spotted, with buttons missing. His wig was always mussed, looking as if it had not been brushed for weeks on end. His mind, soul, energies—all were directed toward the fight against the Crown.

In Hancock, Adams saw a young man who could add money, respectability, and glamor to the Liberty Party. What is more—and Sam Adams was the first to recognize it—Hancock had a personal magnetism which, if properly channeled, could win the hearts of the people. True, at times he had a disturbing tendency toward vanity and arrogance, but there was not a man in Boston more kindhearted or generous, and he had a passionate hatred of injustice.

For his part, John Hancock had never known a man so brilliant as Sam Adams, unless it had been his Uncle Thomas. The shrewdness, canniness, indeed ruthlessness that Thomas Hancock had applied to his business affairs had a surprising counterpart in the qualities Sam Adams brought to bear on politics. John realized that Adams was a man of rare genius, and he threw his weight—and fortune—behind him.

Meanwhile, the first shipment of stamps arrived. Afraid of what would happen if they were brought into Boston, Governor Bernard ordered them landed at Castle William on the island in the Harbor. Hancock immediately dashed off a letter to his influential friends in London. "It is universally determined here never to submit to it and the principal merch[ts] here will by no means carry on Business under a Stamp," he wrote. "The Consequences of its taking place here will be bad,

& attended with many troubles, & I believe may say more fatal to you than us." Then he added, "For God's Sake, use your Interest to relieve us. I dread the Event."

Business affairs called John out of town for a trip southward, and when he returned to Boston in October he found the town in as much of a ferment as ever. November 1 was approaching, the day the Stamp Act was to go into effect, and the townspeople were determined to shut down business completely. "You will find it come to pass that the people of this Country will never Suffer themselves to be made slaves of," John wrote to England. "I am Determin'd as soon as I know that they are Resolv'd to insist on this act to Sell my Stock in Trade & Shut up my Warehouse Doors Thus much I told our Govr the other day."

A week later he wrote again, his temper hotter than ever. "Navigation must cease, and I hope eternally will, rather than submit to so cruel, Grievous and inhuman act. I speak for myself. . . . I will not be a slave. I have a Right to the Libertys & Privileges of the English Constitution, & I as an Englishman will enjoy them."

With a few exceptions, this was the attitude reflected by most Bostonians of the time. Liberty and freedom were the issues, liberty and freedom as Englishmen under the English constitution. The question of independence had not yet been raised, and when it was first raised, men like John Hancock backed away from it.

On November 1, the day the Stamp Act was to go into effect, church bells began to toll at dawn. In the Harbor, ships flew their colors at half-mast. And hanging from the branches of the Liberty Tree were effigies of George Grenville, England's Chancellor of the Exchequer, and John Huske, Member of Parliament. Huske, as a former Bostonian, was especially detested because he had not protested Parliament's injustices to the colonies.

Standing beneath the branches of the Liberty Tree, John Hancock looked at the swinging figures with a pang of anguish. There, easily recognized, was John Huske, a man with whom he had spent many cheerful evenings in London five years ago. The times, he realized, were separating him from some of his dearest and closest friends. Sam Quincy, for one, his boon companion at Harvard, had pulled him aside several times to warn him that James Otis and Sam Adams were dangerous. Next, John thought, Quincy would be warning people against him!

All that day many of the townspeople expected rioting to erupt, but the mob—probably tutored by Sam Adams—had learned discipline and control. At three in the afternoon the effigies were quietly cut down and carted out to the town gallows, where they were hanged and then drawn and quartered. There was no violence, no vandalism.

Even Pope's Day (the Boston version of Guy Fawkes' Day) on November 5 did not provoke the raucous brawling that had become a cherished annual tradition. Instead, once the customary parade was over, the crowd gathered for a "Unity Feast" at the Green Dragon Tavern. After a lavish supper, John Hancock rose to deliver a speech.

At twenty-eight, Hancock was so striking in appearance that strangers in town turned to stare when he strode by. Nearly six feet tall, he looked every inch an aristocrat, from his dressed and powdered wig to his smart pumps of grained leather. With his high forehead, keen and kindly eyes, finely chiseled nose, and determined mouth, he gave an impression of spirited frankness. If his shoulders had a slight stoop, and if he sometimes appeared to have had a bad night's sleep, it was common knowledge that he suffered both from gout and from attacks of an illness that had never been clearly diagnosed.

Now, as he stood before the crowd in the Green Dragon, he betrayed no trace of nervousness. For years, from the time he first had gone to work in his uncle's store, he had had dealings with men such as these, on the wharves and the waterfront, in the markets and streets. Indeed, many of the men sitting around the tables in the Green Dragon owed their livelihood to him. He spoke boldly, passionately, urging that they join together to resist England's new policy of taxation, a policy that would bring ruin upon them all.

The crowd was with him from the start. Here was the wealthiest man in New England, the most important merchant in Boston, a man who could—and often did—dine with the Royal Governor. Instead of being aloof and arrogant, like Thomas Hutchinson or Andrew Oliver, he had chosen to move among them.

When John finished his speech, the crowd roared its approval. A pleased smile crossed Sam Adams's face. The magnetism he had detected in Hancock had proved itself. The handsome young merchant had swayed the oddly assorted gathering.

Adams had still another reason for being pleased: John Hancock paid the bill.

Not long after the feast at the Green Dragon, word began circulating that Andrew Oliver was making overtures to the authorities in England to be reinstated as Stamp Master. On a stormy winter day he was summoned to appear at the Liberty Tree, where he was urged to swear that he would never, directly or indirectly, have anything to do with the hated stamps. In the face of the threatening crowd, he was quick to take the oath.

Sitting in his gray carriage apart from the crowd, John Hancock watched the scene with mingled feelings. He was delighted that Oliver—and the stamps—had suffered a setback. Yet he wondered whether he himself had not been too swept away by the passionate emotions of the past few months. Orderly resistance was one thing, but he could not forget the

torrent of violence that had been unleashed the night Hutchinson's home had been sacked.

In the meantime, all business requiring the use of the tax
stamps had become almost paralyzed, and the courts had
ceased to function. About a week before Christmas the Bostonians assembled at a town meeting to discuss the possibility
of reopening the courts without using the stamps. Hancock,
together with Sam Adams and six other citizens, was named
to prepare a petition to Governor Francis Bernard. As counsel
to present the petition, the meeting appointed James Otis,
Jeremiah Gridley, and John Adams, who was still practicing
law in Braintree. Although Governor Bernard rejected the
petition, the upshot was that the courts did re-open, and soon
other business was being transacted with the excuse that the
stamps were "not available." Indeed, they were not, for the
authorities were afraid to bring them in from Castle William,
where they had been deposited.

John Hancock now took a bold step. Late in December he
sent the *Boston Packet* to sea under the command of Captain
John Marshall. She was the first vessel to venture out of Boston Harbor without a stamped clearance, and there was no
assurance that she would be permitted to clear customs on her
arrival in England. By the *Packet* John dispatched a letter
urging his friends in London to "exert yourself for us, & give
us the good tidings, should the repeal of the act take place."
And, he added, "It will afford more joy to America than any
Circumstance that has or can happen. God grant us the desir'd
event, or we are a gone people."

In the midst of all his political activities Hancock was still
immersed in the problems of his large business. For the whale
oil trade he had built a new ship, the *Liberty*, at a cost of more
than £1,000. His cousin, William Bowes, was on the way to
England for an extended visit, and Hancock sent him off with
a letter of credit for £1,500. From Jonathan Barnard, Han-

cock ordered a shipment of retail goods for a shop he was setting up for his friend and assistant, William Palfrey. And there were supplies to be ordered for the garrisons in Nova Scotia. Then, to add to John's worries, Aunt Lydia became seriously ill.

Early in May the annual election of members to represent Boston in the House of Representatives was held. A story, widely circulated, said that when a pre-election caucus was being held to discuss possible candidates, the name of merchant John Rowe was brought up. Sam Adams, so the story goes, turned his eyes toward the Hancock mansion and asked, "Is there not another John that may do better?"

Whether the story is true or not, at the May election both John Hancock and merchant John Rowe were elected, along with Sam Adams, James Otis, and merchant Thomas Cushing. Hancock had moved another step up the political ladder, and Aunt Lydia, now back on her feet, beamed with joy.

On the afternoon of the election, the plump, earnest young lawyer, John Adams, in from Braintree for a visit, was walking on the mall on the Common, when he met his cousin, Sam Adams. As they strolled across the Common together, John Hancock's big stone house came into view. Pointing to it, Sam said to his cousin, "This town has done a wise thing today." "What?" asked John. "They have made that young man's fortune their own," Sam replied.

At this time John Adams, whose only riches were his brains, tended to be impatient with Hancock, whom he regarded as a man of great wealth and small intellect. Later in life, however, looking back on this period of turmoil, Adams realized the great sacrifices the generous, impulsive young merchant had made.

"No man's property was ever more entirely devoted to the public," he wrote. "The quivering anxiety of the public, under the fearful looking for of the vengeance of king, ministry, and

parliament, compelled him to a constant attendance in the
House; his mind was soon engrossed by public cares, alarms,
and terrors; his business was left to subalterns; his private
affairs neglected, and continued to be so to the end of his life."

Early in 1766 rumors began reaching the colonies that
Parliament was to repeal the Stamp Act. Each new ship from
abroad that reached Boston was eagerly greeted. Finally, on
Friday, May 16, the brigantine *Harrison*, owned by John Hancock, hove into the inner harbor. Her captain, Shubael Coffin,
brought the long-awaited news: a bill for repeal had passed
Parliament and had become effective on the first of May.

The following Monday was set for a day of celebration.
The quiet of dawn was broken by the booming of cannon.
Then the bell of the church nearest the Liberty Tree began
ringing. It was answered by the bells of Christ Church; soon
all the church bells in town were pealing. All day long the
town echoed with the sound of drums beating and guns firing.
The Sons of Liberty paid to have the debtors in prison freed,
and the Liberty Tree was decorated with flags and brilliant
streamers.

On the Common the Sons of Liberty erected a huge, four-
sided pyramid, made of oiled paper and illuminated from
within by 280 lamps. A round box of fireworks was placed
at the top. About a hundred yards from the pyramid another
stage was built for more fireworks.

True to style—and a grand style it was—John Hancock had
been busily preparing for the celebration. All the fifty-four
windows of the Beacon Hill mansion were splendidly illuminated, and on the front lawn a stage was erected for still another display of fireworks, this one at Hancock's own expense.
"For the genteel part of the Town," as the newspapers reported, he gave a lavish banquet, and for the populace he had
hogsheads of Madeira wine set out on the Common. It was a
generous gesture, and it was also good politics.

The fireworks continued until nearly midnight, lighting up the sky for miles around. Then, precisely at midnight, the beating of a drum was heard, and the milling throngs of people scattered toward their homes.

Even Governor Bernard joined in the victory celebration. It looked as if peace had at last come to Boston. "I hope now peace & harmony will prevail," John confided to his London friends. "My best Influence & endeavors to that purpose shall be used. I doubt not but the colonies will make all the grateful Returns in their power."

VIII

☆ ☆ ☆
☆

A Storm Brews . . . and the Liberty *Is Seized*

Despite the repeal of the Stamp Act, the disputes between Governor Bernard and the House of Representatives continued. In late May, 1766, Bernard vetoed the election of James Otis as speaker of the House, and the House retaliated by keeping Thomas Hutchinson and Andrew Oliver from becoming members of the Council. At about the same time the Liberty Party was instrumental in having a gallery built in the Town House so that the debates of the House of Representatives could be open to the public.

John Hancock, although increasingly troubled by ill health and by the stagnation in trade, turned his attention back to the competition with William Rotch of Nantucket. In November he boasted to his London associates, "I have now so well established in those concerns in the Whale Fishery that I can have the refusal of almost all their oyl & I think Mr. R——h has had small success in purchasing & by far the greatest quantity of oyl will be in your hands which is my aim." He expected to get a good price for the cargo, and he got it.

His life was more hectic than ever. "I have been & still am

so excessively hurried," he confessed to Jonathan Barnard, "that I have scarcely time to sleep, what with attending court in the House of Assembly, my own store & ships in and out. Whalemen fitting out for the West Indies & all my oyle men with open mouths gaping for money. I have enough to do, but you & I love hurry which will be my lot while I live."

The year 1767 brought him even more hurry. In May he was re-elected to the House of Representatives, polling 618 votes, proving himself a better vote-getter than Samuel Adams and James Otis, re-elected with 574 votes each, and Thomas Cushing with 557. Behind the scenes, Otis and Adams were still the prime movers, but in the public eye the friendly, courtly young merchant was making rapid headway as a politician. Hancock took huge delight in his growing popularity.

This year also brought the Townshend Acts, levying import duties on glass, lead, paints, paper, and tea, as well as establishing an American Board of Commissioners of the Customs at Boston, directly responsible to the British Treasury Board. Hancock and the other Boston merchants were roused to fury. At a session of the town meeting just before Christmas, the Boston representatives in the House were instructed to propose non-importation of British goods, especially luxury items.

Meanwhile, a series of "Letters from a Farmer in Pennsylvania to the Inhabitants of the British Colonies" had begun to appear in the newspapers, arguing that the Townshend Acts were unconstitutional and that Parliament did not have the right to impose taxes in order to raise a revenue in America. At a town meeting in March, 1768, Hancock and Sam Adams were two members of a committee of five appointed to prepare a letter of thanks to the "Farmer," John Dickinson of Pennsylvania.

As a result of the Townshend Acts, additional customs commissioners were sent to Boston. They proved a constant irritation to the townspeople. Finally John Hancock rose in the

House of Representatives. He would not, he declared, allow any of the customs officials "to go even on board any of his London ships."

He soon was given the opportunity to make good his threat. On April 7, 1768, the *Lydia*, commanded by Captain James Scott, dropped anchor in Boston Harbor after a voyage from London. That afternoon two customs officials, known as tide-waiters, boarded the vessel to watch for tea, paper, or any other goods subject to duty. (Under the law there was a difference between "watching" for goods and "searching" for goods.) Word of the boarding was carried swiftly to the hot-tempered merchant-politician, who rushed down to the wharf, confronted the tidewaiters, and demanded to see their papers. He told Captain Scott that the tidewaiters might stay aboard to watch, but they were not, under any circumstances, to go below decks to search. Intimidated by the ship-owner's fiery manner—and by the muttering crowd that had gathered—the tidewaiters departed.

The following night, however, one of the two, Owen Richards, slipped on board the *Lydia* about eleven o'clock and made his way down into the hold. As soon as the interloper was discovered, Hancock was notified. Marching down to the wharf with eight or ten supporters, the owner of the *Lydia* ordered the mates to drag Richards up on deck. There he faced the tidewaiter and demanded his authority to search. Richards could produce no writ of assistance. Hancock asked explicitly if he wished to "search" the ship. Half frightened out of his wits, Richards replied that he did not. Even when told that he might search every part of the *Lydia* except the hold, he refused, and departed in a flurry, before the burly mates could throw him off the vessel.

Hancock had been very careful to keep within the bounds of the law, yet the Customs Board tried to make an example of him. Even when the attorney general upheld his actions, the

Board insisted on sending the papers on to the Treasury in London. Here, too, the Board met with failure. The Treasury decided that Hancock's defiance had been within his rights.

Before long the customs officers had their revenge. On May 9 the *Liberty*, Nathaniel Bernard, Master, arrived in port with a cargo including wine from Madeira. As with the *Lydia*, two tidewaiters boarded her to be sure that no cargo subject to duty was put ashore without payment of the proper fees. The next day a report was entered at the Custom House that twenty-five casks of wine were among the cargo, and the duty was paid. When the tidewaiters were questioned, they insisted that no wine had been smuggled off. There, for the time being, the matter rested.

A week later the 50-gun British frigate *Romney*, short of men, dropped anchor in Boston Harbor. When seamen from other vessels were pressed into service aboard the *Romney*, the citizens of Boston were blind with rage. The merchants were incensed for another reason: they believed that the customs officials had called for the *Romney* to help enforce the new revenue laws.

Meanwhile, the sloop *Liberty* lay at Clark's Wharf, now generally called Hancock's Wharf, taking on an outgoing cargo of twenty barrels of tar and two hundred barrels of whale oil. Although regulations required that a bond be posted and a cargo list filed before a vessel was loaded, it had become a common custom to post bond and file the cargo list just before the ship was ready to sail. Hancock followed this common custom, and here he made a disastrous mistake. On June 10, a few days before the *Liberty* was to sail, the customs officials seized the vessel for loading without a permit. The customs officers were jubilant; they were going to teach that scoundrel Hancock a lesson!

On the same day that the *Liberty* was seized, Thomas Kirk, one of the tidewaiters who had originally boarded her back in

May, went to his superiors with an astounding story. On the night of May 9, he said, soon after he and his companion started their inspection, John Marshall, captain of another of Hancock's ships, came on board the *Liberty* with a gang of ruffians. Marshall asked Kirk if he would consent to their unloading a number of casks of wine without entering them at the Custom House the next day. When Kirk firmly refused, Marshall and his gang dragged the tidewaiter down into the cabin and nailed up the companionway.

For three hours Kirk paced about in the cabin, listening to the tumult on the deck above and the creaking of the tackle. Although he could not see what was going on, he was certain that cargo was being hoisted out upon the wharf. Smuggling was being done within his earshot, and he was powerless to prevent it.

Finally, when quiet reigned on deck, Marshall had the companionway freed and appeared in the cabin. If Kirk breathed one word of what had happened, Marshall said, his life would be in danger and his property destroyed. The tidewaiter fled home.

As Hancock and his supporters were quick to point out, Kirk's story had several obvious weaknesses. One was that Captain Marshall—who had dropped dead the morning after the alleged smuggling—was in no position to deny Kirk's accusations. Moreover the second tidewaiter could not confirm the tale. He said he had fallen asleep after boarding the *Liberty*. Kirk insisted he had been drunk and gone home to bed.

Nevertheless, the officers of the Crown rejoiced. On two counts, they thought, they had John Hancock exactly where they wanted him. First, his sloop *Liberty* would be forfeited because the cargo list had not been filed; second, Hancock himself stood accused of smuggling. "The richest man in the Country and the Known Abettor of Tumultuous proceedings," as they called him, was about to get his just desserts.

But they reckoned without the Boston mob. Quite a crowd collected on the wharf when it was heard that Joseph Harrison, Collector of the Port, and Benjamin Hallowell, Comptroller of the Customs, had ordered the "broad arrow" painted on the *Liberty*, denoting that she had been seized. Harrison felt it safe to leave the *Liberty* at the wharf, but Hallowell insisted that she be placed under the guns of the *Romney*, a quarter-mile offshore. Boats from the man-of-war came in, cut the *Liberty*'s moorings, and began to tow her away.

The crowd flew into a frenzy, hurling insults at Harrison and Hallowell, and threatening to throw the *Romney*'s crew overboard. Despite some violence on the wharf, the men from the *Romney* got the *Liberty* out into the Harbor. Then the mob, by now about five hundred strong, turned on the two customs officials. As they fled, bricks were hurled at them. Hands reached out and ripped their coats. Harrison's son was seized and dragged along the ground by the hair of his head.

The mob was now completely out of control. Many of the brawling, shouting men had no idea what they were fighting about. Some of them believed the riot has started over an attempt by the *Romney*'s crew to impress landsmen.

Hancock made it a point to keep his distance from the wharf. It was one thing to stand up for his rights; it was quite another matter to incite a riot. He would argue his case in the courts, not in the streets. Besides, he knew his own quick temper. If he went down to the wharf, he might become as infuriated as any member of the mob. So he paced the carpet of the Beacon Hill drawing room, while Aunt Lydia tried to calm him.

The mob, having left the customs officials bruised and bleeding on the wharf, proceeded to rampage through the town. At the house of Inspector General Williams, they broke all the windows. Then they attacked Hallowell's home. Their final gesture was to seize a pleasure boat belonging to Harrison, drag it through the streets to the Common, and burn it almost before John Hancock's door, as if they were pagans making a sacrifice to their god.

Watching the flames out of the drawing room window, Hancock could not suppress a smile of satisfaction. But still he was careful not to show his face. Any sign that he sanctioned the rioting might provoke the mob to new violence.

The next day, Saturday, Boston was quiet. Harrison, approached by some of Hancock's representatives, agreed to return the *Liberty* if the merchant would give his bond to redeliver her when the case was heard in the Admiralty Court. Indeed, Harrison even sent Hancock a note stating that he would accept merely Hancock's word as security. Harrison and Hallowell now regarded this aspect of the matter settled.

The note was a signal for a conclave of the Whig leaders. The Boston Whigs, most of them members of the Liberty Party, opposed the policies of Parliament, whereas the Tories, or Loyalists, supported these policies.

That Sunday evening coach after coach rattled up Beacon Hill to the Hancock gate. Sam Adams came, wearing the same old rusty coat and smiling triumphantly at the course events were taking. The hulking, fiery James Otis arrived, uttering fearful oaths as he clumped up the stone steps. At forty-three he was proving as much a threat to his friends as to his enemies. Fits of insanity struck him like lightning. At his best he was unstable; one moment he would denounce King George III; the next, Sam Adams. After James Otis came Dr. Joseph Warren, now twenty-seven, four years younger than Hancock. Lively, volatile, enthusiastic, Joseph Warren had become as expert at practicing politics as he was at practicing medicine.

Gathered in the long drawing room, which was brilliantly illuminated by dozens of wax candles, the men debated in low, serious voices. Amid the mirrors, silver, gleaming floors and mahogany of the elegant room, Sam Adams seemed more shabby than ever, but his presence was a dominating force in the group.

The debate went on for hours. Otis, in one of his conciliatory moods, urged compromise: Hancock should accept Harrison's offer. It was, Otis felt, generous in the extreme. Adams and Warren counseled a more agressive course: defiance of Harrison and Hallowell.

Their host—whose property was at stake—paced up and down the room, his face white and drawn. He had been ill lately, troubled by severe headaches. Whatever decision he made now would have far-reaching effects, and his heart was troubled. If he agreed to the terms of Harrison's note, he might regain the *Liberty*. Yet he was willing to take the risk of losing her if it meant striking a blow at the revenue officials.

The meeting broke up shortly before midnight. On his way home, Dr. Warren stopped by Hallowell's home to deliver Hancock's answer: the merchant would have no part of any compromise with the customs officials.

(As it turned out, Hancock never regained possession of the *Liberty*. Two stories, both with the same ironic twist, have circulated as to her fate: that she was the revenue cutter *Liberty* stranded off Goat Island in 1769 and burned by Newport patriots, and that she became the revenue cutter *Gaspée*, boarded and burned by Providence patriots in 1772.)

The ill will aroused by the presence of the *Romney* in the Harbor and by the *Liberty* affair was still evident in the stormy expressions of the townspeople. The customs officials went about in fear for their lives; threats and abuse were hurled at them every time they ventured out in the streets. On Monday, unable to stand the strain any longer, they fled with their families aboard the *Romney*; eventually they took refuge in Castle William on the island in Boston Harbor.

Tempers were hot; the Sons of Liberty were ready to strike. A meeting at the Liberty Tree was called for ten o'clock Tuesday morning. Despite a pouring rain, several thousand townsmen turned out and then adjourned to Faneuil Hall. Hancock and other moderates, sensing that the slightest spark could set off a blaze of rioting, urged recourse to the traditional forum for orderly protest: the town meeting. At three o'clock that afternoon hordes of citizens turned out for the town meeting, which was held in Old South Church. There it was voted to send a petition to Governor Bernard requesting that the *Romney* be ordered out of the Harbor.

Twenty-one men were appointed to carry the request to Bernard, among them Hancock, Otis, Warren, Sam Adams, and Joseph Jackson, father of the pert young Sally John Hancock still courted despite Aunt Lydia's frowns. At the moment, Governor Bernard was staying at his summer home, four miles out of town on the southwest shore of Jamaica Pond. The committee of twenty-one, in a splendid procession of eleven chaises, set out from the grand stone house on Beacon Hill, John Hancock leading, with James Otis at his side.

For once, Francis Bernard was tactful. Greeting the committee as gentlemen, not scoundrels, he invited them into his home and ordered servants to bring wine. After listening courteously to their request, he said he would give an answer in writing the next day. More wine was passed around, and the committee left, congratulating themselves on the success of their mission.

Bernard had no intention of complying with their petition. Although the reply he sent to the town meeting the following day was phrased in conciliatory terms, he promised nothing. Instead, he dispatched secret letters to General Gage in New York and Admiral Hood in Halifax, requesting military assistance in keeping order in the town. And a day or so later he wrote to England, "If there was not a revolt, the leaders of the Sons of Liberty must falsify their words and change their purposes; yet I cannot think they will be so mad as to attempt to defend the Town, in its defenceless state, against the King's forces." Then he added, "But the lengths they have gone already are scarce short of madness."

Bernard's next step, taken July 1, was to dissolve the General Court, comprised of the Council and House of Representatives. The Boston merchants retaliated in August by adopting a stringent resolution not to import any of the items to which the Townshend duties applied, starting January 1, 1769.

In September, Hancock, Sam Adams, Dr. Warren, and four others were appointed by the town meeting to meet with Governor Bernard to request that he call a new General Court. When Bernard refused, the Bostonians summoned an informal Provincial Congress of their own, to which ninety-six Massachusetts towns sent delegates. Hancock, Otis, Samuel Adams, and Thomas Cushing were appointed to represent Boston. Aside from drawing up a petition to request relief from unfair taxation and military oppression, the convention conducted little business, yet it was significant as a unified gesture by the entire province.

"It is a great grief to this people that they are Deprived of the Benefits of a General Assembly, more especially at this time, when there is need of the wisdom of the whole Province to conduct our Public affairs," Hancock informed his London friend and business associate, George Haley. "I am confident the Convention of these Committees had a happy Effect, to quiet the minds of the people, but . . . I dare say they will be much misrepresented. Everything here has been conducted with the greatest order on the part of the people, and I can't but hope that when things are really known in England, we shall be relieved. I pray & doubt not of Your Influence for us."

In his own mind, John Hancock was very clear as to his position. He had allied himself, financially and politically, with Sam Adams and Joseph Warren, who were self-acknowledged radicals. In opposing the search of the *Lydia* he had probably been the first citizen of wealth and position to lead physical resistance to officers of the Crown. In the *Liberty* affair he had stood up against what he considered grossly unfair revenue laws. But, and this he firmly believed, the Bostonians were "as loyal as any in the King's Domain," and he was one of the most loyal Bostonians. What he fought for were his rights as an Englishman.

No sooner had the Provincial Convention broken up than twelve British warships sailed into Boston Harbor and dropped anchor. On October 1, at high noon, three regiments of infantry and a train of artillery landed at Long Wharf. With bayonets fixed, drums beating, and fifes playing, nearly a thousand redcoats marched through King Street and on to Boston Common, where they staged a drill to impress the hordes of townspeople who had assembled. One regiment set up camp on the Common, within sight of the Hancock mansion; a second was quartered in Faneuil Hall; and the third, together with the train of artillery, was scattered, part in the Town House, the rest in stores along Griffin's Wharf.

"The Report of the Troops coming here alarmed the people much," John Hancock advised friends in London, "& more especially as we were patiently waiting . . . but unused as we are to troops & notwithstanding the apprehensions of people & such a number of troops in this Town, the people are quiet and peaceful and not the least Disturbance has taken place."

The quiet was only momentary. About a week after the arrival of the troops, a large guardhouse built on "The Neck" was pulled down in the dead of night. Governor Bernard offered a reward for the culprits, but no one came forward. The townspeople began to complain of being insulted and abused by the soldiers. The Town Watch were accosted during their rounds. Brawls broke out in the taverns. Thefts increased. Whether or not the redcoats actually were to blame, the people of Boston held them accountable.

Now the town had a new cause for grievance. On Novem-

ber 3 their most prominent merchant, John Hancock, was
placed under arrest as the result of a suit filed by Attorney
General Jonathan Sewall on instructions from England. Sewall
was Dolly Quincy's brother-in-law, and the revival of the
Liberty affair embarrassed him as much as it incensed others.
A judgment was being asked against Hancock for £9,000
sterling, treble the value of the cargo of wine allegedly smuggled into town the previous May. A like judgment was asked
against five supposed accomplices. At first the Marshal of the
Court refused to set Hancock free on bail, but finally released
him on the payment of the fantastic sum of £3,000 ready
money.

When the case came up before the Court of Vice-Admiralty, Hancock retained as defense counsel his old acquaintance
from Braintree and Harvard, the rising young lawyer, John
Adams. The trial dragged on all through the winter, becoming a "painful Drudgery" to Adams and to everyone else connected with it. The Crown seemed determined to interrogate
practically everyone in Boston; they even threatened to call
Aunt Lydia to the stand, but the stoutest officials probably
quailed before that prospect. No matter how many witnesses
were called, the Crown could make no headway. Wholesale
perjury was the order of the day, every day. To hear the testimony, one would think that every soul in Boston had been
sound asleep on the night in question.

Even John Adams was able to make little progress for the
defense, although he presented some arguments that were to
echo and re-echo in the years to come. Hancock, he said, had
never voted for the revenue law he was accused of violating.
Nor had he voted for any of the men who made the law. The
issue of taxation without representation was a good one, and
Adams made the most of it. Moreover, since the case was heard
before a single judge, Adams inserted a few pointed remarks

about the denial of the traditional right of all Englishmen to trial by jury.

On and on and on the trial went, until Adams himself was "thoroughly weary and disgusted with the Court, the Officers of the Crown, the Cause, and even with the tyrranical Bell that dongled me out of my House every Morning." At last, on March 26, 1769, the Crown abandoned the case. It was moved that the prosecution of Hancock and his friends be retracted. And across the record was written: "Our Sovereign Lord the King will prosecute no further hereon." In the eyes of the people Hancock emerged as a hero and a symbol of resistance to oppression.

IX

☆ ☆ ☆

☆

The Bloody Scuffle in King Street . . . and a Party on Griffin's Wharf

Not everyone admired John Hancock; the Tories detested him, and even Sam and John Adams were to find themselves at odds with him. The Tories were incensed because, to them, he had betrayed his class, thrown in his lot with the rabble when he should have followed in the steps of Uncle Thomas, steps that never wavered from the path of loyalty. Both Sam and John Adams acted according to the dictates of their heads; Hancock was more likely to listen to his heart. Moreover, he had a tendency to try to please everyone among his friends, with the result that he sometimes pleased none of them. But what irked his political foes and political friends alike was his swashbuckling manner, his flair for taking the center of the stage, and, most important, his tremendous, overwhelming popularity with the people. All Hancock had to do was drive by in his splendid carriage, and the crowds would cheer. He was their favorite, and the Adamses often went unnoticed. When some of the people fondly began to call him "King"

Hancock, it was hard to tell whether Thomas Hutchinson or Samuel Adams was the more infuriated.

No one among the Liberty Party, however, denied that John Hancock was essential to their cause. Here was a man everyone would have expected to be a Tory, a man of wealth, prestige, and the utmost respectability. If Aunt Lydia had hoped he might be Governor, her hopes were not without foundation. Yet he threw his wealth, his energy, his personal magnetism into the struggle, and he attracted the aid of many men who would never have followed Sam Adams alone. From the Liberty Party he could gain almost nothing compared to what he stood to achieve as a Tory—nothing except the satisfaction of doing what he believed was right.

His prominence made him a special object of vilification by the Tories. While he was on trial for the *Liberty* affair, a letter appeared in the paper charging that he had written to General Thomas Gage in New York, suggesting that the Hancock store provision the British troops soon to arrive in Boston. Hancock rushed to deny the accusation: "If such a letter has been produced I declare it to be a forgery; for I have never made application to any for the supply of said troops, nor did I ever desire any person to do it for me. The person who produced the letter could have no other design but to injure my reputation, and abuse the gentlemen of New York."

In May, 1769, he was re-elected a Representative, along with his friends Otis, Cushing, and Samuel Adams; and he was active in the next session of the General Court in pushing for the withdrawal of troops. This issue, in fact, consumed so much time that very little other business was done while the General Court was in session. Governor Bernard refused to do anything about removing the troops; instead, he removed the General Court from Boston to Cambridge, a step that inflamed Hancock and the moderates as much as it did Sam Adams and the radicals. The will of the colonists as opposed to the will of

A View of the Hancock Mansion from Boston Common. From an engraving in the *Massachusetts Magazine*, July, 1789.

John Hancock. From the John Hancock Mutual Life Insurance Company's copy of the portrait by John Singleton Copley, held by the Museum of Fine Arts, Boston, on deposit from the City of Boston.

Thomas Hancock. Portrait by John Singleton Copley.

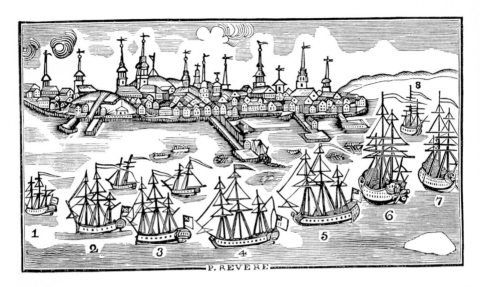

The Landing of the British Troops at Boston in 1768. Long Wharf is in the center, Hancock's Wharf to the right. From an 1856 copy of Paul Revere's engraving for *Edes and Gill's North American Almanack and Massachusetts Register for the Year 1770.*

Harvard College in the Early Eighteenth Century. From an old copy of William Burgis's engraving, "A Prospect of the Colledges in Cambridge in New England."

Samuel Adams. From the original picture by Chappel.

The Boston Tea Party. From *Ballou's Pictorial Drawing-Room Companion.*

The Boston Massacre. From *Ballou's Pictorial Drawing-Room Companion.*

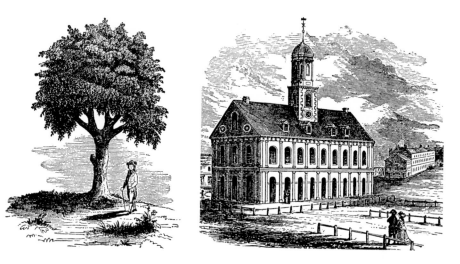

The Liberty Tree and Faneuil Hall. From Drake's *Old Landmarks of Boston*.

The Battle of Lexington. From the original picture by Chappel.

John Adams. From the engraving by Ste-
phenson after a painting by Copley.

Joseph Warren. From the original picture by Chappel.

Independence Hall (the Pennsylvania State House) in 1776. From the engraving by John C. McRae.

Dorothy Quincy. From the portrait by John Singleton Copley.

John Hancock and his wife, Dorothy Quincy Hancock, by Edward Savage.
In the Collection of The Corcoran Gallery of Art; bequest of Woodbury
Blair.

Courtesy of the John Hancock Mutual Life Insurance Company

John Hancock's Defiance. From the lithograph by Currier & Ives, 1876.

Signing of the Declaration of Independence. From the John Hancock Mutual Life Insurance Company's copy by Griswold Tyng of the painting by John Trumbull in the Yale University Art Gallery.

The Announcement of the Declaration of Independence. From the engraving by J. Mc Goffin.

John Hancock's Signature on John Paul Jones's Commission as Captain and on a Document Appointing Jones to Command the *Providence*.

John Hancock. From the original picture by Chappel.

the Royal Governor now became an issue in the growing controversy.

Ill will simmered throughout the summer and into the fall. Hancock fumed at the stubborn Governor's adamant refusal to make the slightest gesture to relieve the growing tension. Then, early in August, Bernard sailed to England for a visit, leaving Lieutenant Governor Hutchinson in charge. Soon after this, Hancock and the merchants decided to reinforce their non-importation agreement by publishing the names of the violators in the newspapers. Among those held up to disgrace were Bernard's son and two sons of Hutchinson.

August 14 would mark the fourth anniversary of the birth of the Sons of Liberty. Preparations were made for a rousing celebration, chiefly underwritten by John Hancock. No one in Boston took greater zest in festivities than he did, especially on such an occasion as this, which promised to be one that Bostonians would remember for decades to come.

Not so eager was lawyer John Adams, who went only because he felt it his duty. "If I had been absent," he confessed, "many might suspect that I was not hearty in the cause."

On the morning of the anniversary, the Sons of Liberty and the Whig leaders, some 350 stalwart men in all, assembled in the shade of the Liberty Elm and drank fourteen toasts, starting with salutes to the King, Queen, and Royal family. The crowd then tumbled into carriages or mounted horses and rode out to Robinson's Tavern, "at the sign of the Liberty Tree," in Dorchester, away from the curious eyes of the British troops in Boston. Leading the procession was the splendid chariot of the merchant prince of Beacon Hill, John Hancock, Esquire.

In Dorchester, tables were spread in a field by the tavern, with a huge awning over them, to protect the celebrants from the heat of the sun. Three large barbecued pigs and a host of other provisions had been prepared for the banquet, which started at two o'clock. Music was played; ballads were sung; cannon were fired; and, after dinner, forty-five toasts were drunk. By five o'clock the celebration was over. A procession of 139 carriages, "King" Hancock again leading the parade, rolled back into Boston. The cavalcade moved through the streets to the Town House, passed around it, and then parted, each of the Sons of Liberty going to his own home, quietly, orderly, and, according to John Adams, soberly.

The celebration had been a shrewd move on the part of Hancock and Sam Adams. As John Adams observed, such festivities "tinge the Minds of the People, they impregnate them with the sentiments of Liberty. They render the People fond of their Leaders in the Cause, and averse and bitter against all opposers."

As winter came on, John Hancock was increasingly in-volved in the efforts to enforce non-importation, even though the policy had brought his own once-thriving business almost to a standstill. "I am wholly engaged in the accommodation of the late Importations," he wrote to George Haley in London, "made here by Several Persons of this Town, which circum-stances taking place at the only important moment that it should have been avoided, I must say Reflects great on the Importers." Haley, too, was at fault. "It gives me great un-easiness on your acct. that almost the whole of the goods that have arrived have been shipped by you . . . . it is a most un-lucky thing."

With the dawn of 1770 one unpleasant incident began to follow another. In February a government informer, Ebenezer Richardson, engaged in a street squabble with some boys. When they began hurling stones at him, he retreated to his house and, in a panic, fired a gun from a window, severely wounding one boy and killing another. The victim, only eleven years old, was given a splendid funeral by the Sons of Liberty, who were not likely to overlook the propaganda value of the event. Richardson was found guilty of murder, but Hutchinson, viewing the deed as justifiable homicide, refused to sign the death warrant. This did not increase Hutchinson's popularity with his fellow Bostonians.

Toward the end of February, several other street fights broke out, and close to noon on Friday, March 2, there was a pitched battle between several soldiers and the ropemakers at John Gray's Ropewalk. Although no one suffered seriously, word spread that trouble was brewing. Soldiers and civilians alike were spoiling for a battle.

About nine o'clock the night of March 5, two young Bostonians on their way home got into a scuffle with a sentinel on watch. Almost at once a crowd collected; soldiers were called out to disperse them. In the fighting that followed, the soldiers were forced to retreat to their barracks in Brattle Street. The mob now turned its attention to the Main Guard, stationed in King Street opposite the Town House.

Before reaching the Town House, however, the mob fell upon the sentinel at the Custom House, who retreated up the steps under a shower of snowballs, pieces of ice, oyster shells, and sticks of wood. Terrified, unable to open the door and escape, the sentinel called for the Main Guard.

Meanwhile, bells had begun tolling, drawing even larger crowds into King Street. The Guard, pressed upon by the mob, formed a half-circle, bayonets fixed. In the confusion that followed, the order to fire was heard. One after another, seven or eight muskets fired. When the smoke cleared away, five bodies lay on the icy street, their blood staining the snow. Three were dead—Crispus Attucks, a mulatto; Samuel Gray, one of the ropewalk men; and James Caldwell, a mate from one of the vessels in the harbor. The next morning seventeen-year-old Samuel Maverick died. Patrick Carr lingered on for four days.

As the crowd dragged its dead away, more soldiers poured

out of the barracks. All over the city bells were ringing wildly. It seemed that every citizen of Boston was now in the streets. Rushing to the Town House, Lieutenant Governor Hutchinson addressed the surging throng from the balcony, urging them to disperse, that the law would take its course. The soldiers who had fired into the crowd were placed under arrest; then, slowly, the crowd began to scatter.

One of many things about the night of March 5 that was never explained was the identity of a mysterious gentleman who appeared in Dock Square to address the crowd. He was described as a tall man in a white wig and red cloak. Stories differed as to what he said, the Loyalists claiming he had spurred the mob on to violence, the Patriots protesting that he had advised the people to return to their homes. No one ever revealed exactly who he was. Some suggested Sam Adams, yet Adams was only of medium height. Others pointed out that John Hancock stood six feet tall; could he have been the man in the red cloak? One of the soldiers identified the figure as a Whig named William Molineux.

To a Loyalist, Samuel Adams wrote, "As it is not known what the tall gentleman with the red cloak said to the people, whether he gave them good or ill advice, or any advice at all, we may probably form some conjecture concerning it when his person is ascertained." His person never was "ascertained." The Sons of Liberty kept the secret well.

But the Sons were quick to seize on the shooting of the five men and spread the news throughout the colonies. A "bloody massacre," they called it, and the Boston Massacre was widely condemned as a deed of monumental British infamy. Here and there, however, a few calm voices spoke out, declaring that the British soldiers had been goaded beyond endurance by the Boston mob.

The morning following the Massacre a Boston town meeting was hastily summoned, and it was voted that the people and the soldiers could no longer live together in the town. John Hancock—who had become a symbol of resistance to tyranny ever since the *Liberty* affair—was appointed chairman of a committee of fifteen to demand the removal of the troops. When the group called on Hutchinson, the Lieutenant Governor replied that he had no such authority. Then a committee of seven, including Hancock, Sam Adams, Warren, and Molineux, confronted Hutchinson again. At last the Lieutenant Governor gave way, agreeing to transfer the troops to Castle William.

As the troops were preparing to depart, Colonel Dalrymple came to see Chairman Hancock. He feared, he said, that the troops would be attacked. Would Hancock delegate one member of the committee to march with the troops as a guarantee of their safety? Hancock agreed, appointing Molineux, who, if he was the tall gentleman in the red cloak, proved an ironical bodyguard for the troops.

The Sons of Liberty made the funeral of the victims a ceremony the town would not soon forget. Shops were closed; bells tolled. The hearses joined at the spot in King Street where the Massacre had taken place, and the mourners then paraded through the streets of Boston, followed by the carriages of the town's most distinguished citizens, John Hancock prominent among them.

Pressures were beginning to take their toll of the merchant-politician. Non-importation made any attempt to carry on business an unceasing series of headaches. Then there had been the *Lydia* and *Liberty* incidents, and his never-ending duties as a member of the House and one of the Boston selectmen. His brother Ebenezer was a problem, too. Although John had helped establish him in business, he was going heavily into debt; at any moment John feared that Eben would be bankrupt. The gout was giving him increasing trouble, and he was often forced to take to his bed when he should have been up and about. If he could stop trying to be all things to all men, he would be better off, but an overeagerness to please was his greatest weakness.

On April 18, 1770, he was chosen Speaker of the House *pro tempore;* Hutchinson, bitterly opposed to him, vetoed the appointment. In May John, close to nervous exhaustion, was re-elected to the House, once again polling more votes than his running mates, Sam Adams, Cushing, and James Bowdoin.

The election precipitated a crisis. Word reached Hancock that certain factions among the Sons of Liberty were reviling him, perhaps out of resentment that James Otis had not been one of those elected. Already overworked, John gave way to his irritation and threatened to resign. Sam Adams rushed into the breach, attempting to repair the damage. Hancock was too essential a figure to be lost to the Liberty Party; no one realized this more than Adams.

"Your Resolution," he wrote to John, "gave me very great Uneasiness. I could not think you had sufficient Ground to deprive the Town of one whom I have a Right to say is a most valuable Member. . . . Those who were fond of continuing Mr Otis on the Seat, were I dare say to a Man among your warmest friends: Will you then add to their Disappointment by a Resignation, merely because one contemptible person, who perhaps was hired for the purpose, has blessed you with his *reviling*. . . ."

Adams's entreaty was successful; Hancock was sworn in with the other Representatives. Once again Hutchinson insisted on holding the General Court in Cambridge, which obliged Merchant Hancock to be absent from Boston more often than he wished. Business was still not good, but what there was he had to entrust to his assistant, Palfrey. He did have hopes that things would grow better. Earlier in the year all the Townshend duties except the one on tea had been repealed, and the non-importation agreements were drawing to a close. In June he showed optimism in a letter to one of the English firms with which he did business, "I hope e'er long matters will be so settled as that trade may revive, do convince your noble gentlemen at Helm of the ill consequences of a perseverance in their present measures. . . . It is a true saying 'Oppression will make a wise man mad.'"

On into the fall of 1770 the Liberty Party continued to squabble with Hutchinson, although the removal of troops from the town had relieved much of the tension. In November, however, the House took a step that was to have important consequences for the future. John Hancock, Samuel and John Adams, and two others were appointed "a committee of correspondence to communicate such intelligence as may be necessary to the agent [the agent, or representative, for Massachusetts in England was now Benjamin Franklin] and others in Great Britain, and also to the Speakers of the several Assemblies through the continent, or to such committee of correspondence as they have or may appoint." The committees of correspondence were to play an influential part in bringing the colonies together in their opposition to the Crown.

For Thomas Hutchinson, the beginning of 1771 seemed the dawn of a new, and brighter, era. "We have not been so quiet these five years," he boasted to friends in England. "The people about the country have certainly altered their conduct, and in this town, if it were not for two or three Adamses, we should do well enough." No doubt he considered John Hancock as one of the "three Adamses."

In March Hutchinson was appointed Governor of Massachusetts, replacing Bernard. His brother-in-law, Andrew Oliver, became Lieutenant Governor. And the Governor's salary was henceforth to be paid directly by the Crown, rather than by the Massachusetts legislature, the General Court—thus removing the Province's main weapon against a Royal Governor: the power to withhold his salary.

But what pleased Hutchinson even more were signs of disaffection among the members of the Liberty Party. Opposition to the Crown was weakening. John Adams had given up public office and returned to Braintree. Even though the May elections had returned Sam Adams, Cushing, Otis, and Hancock to the House, Otis was on the brink of complete insanity, and there were signs of a growing breach between Sam Adams and Hancock.

When the House suggested Hancock as one of the members of the Governor's Council, Hutchinson vetoed his appointment, as he had done several times in the past. "I was much pressed by many persons well affected in general to consent to the election of Mr. Hancock," Hutchinson admitted. "They assured me he wished to be separated from Mr. Adams, another Representative of the town, an incendiary equal to any at present in London. . . . As there had been no advances on his part, I could not think it proper for me to follow their advice. I have now reason to think that, before another election, he will alter his conduct so far as to justify my acceptance of him. . . ."

Before long, the thin, lean Governor and the handsome, elegant merchant met for a private interview. Hancock confessed dissatisfaction with the Liberty Party, expressing dislike of their "extending their designs further than appeared to him warrantable." This was just the opening Hutchinson had been looking for. He assured Hancock that he bore him no personal ill will, that all would be forgotten and forgiven if the merchant would guarantee his loyalty to the Crown—and to the Governor. Hutchinson now held forth what he thought would be tempting bait: he offered to accept him as a member of the Council, where, as Hutchinson phrased it, "he could more easily take such share in the public affairs as he thought fit, than he could do in the House, business in the latter requiring a more close and constant attention."

Hancock, however, was not to be tempted. He bluntly informed the Governor that he did not wish to be a Council member. Indeed, he intended to quit public affairs and devote his attention to his long-neglected private business.

Nevertheless, Hutchinson refused to give up hope of winning him over to the Tory side. In October the Governor gleefully told Bernard, "Hancock and Adams are at great variance. Some of my friends blow the coals, and I hope to see a good effect." Hutchinson also had what was, to him, even more pleasing news to report to Bernard: "Otis was carried off to-day in a post-chaise, bound hand and foot. He has been as good as his word,—set the Province in a flame, and perished in the attempt."

Hancock's split with Sam Adams was caused as much by illness and private worries as it was by disapproval of the extremes to which Adams's politics were taking him. Eben Hancock had gone bankrupt, and his older brother was helping him get back on his feet. Ordering supplies from England, he specified, "These goods are for my brother, whom I am determined to establish in Business again in hopes he may better succeed, & over whom I shall be careful to keep a watchful eye." John himself had been so sick for months as to be unable to attend properly to his own affairs, let alone Eben's. Early in November, however, he began to show signs of improvement. "I am so surprisingly Recover'd," he joyfully announced to George Haley, "that I have plunged myself in the Business of Life again."

But the estrangement from Sam Adams continued. In January, 1772, Hutchinson informed Bernard that "The faction seems to be breaking. . . . Hancock has not been with their Club for two months past, and seems to have a new set of acquaintance. . . . His coming over will be a great loss to them, as they support themselves with his money." Hutchinson was still making every attempt to win Hancock to his side. A

highly intelligent man and an astute politician, the Governor
was, as Sam Adams pointed out, able to "smile sweetly, even
upon the man he hates," and these days he was smiling as
sweetly as he could upon John Hancock. When the General
Court assembled in April, Hancock was chosen Speaker of the
House, and the appointment was accepted by Hutchinson.

For all his wiles, Hutchinson was unsuccessful. In May,
after the annual election of Representatives, Hancock was
one of those put forward for the Council, meeting Hutchinson's
approval. Much to the Governor's surprise and chagrin, Hancock refused the appointment. Realizing that the enmity between Hancock and Adams had gone far enough, their mutual
friends had brought about a reconciliation. To celebrate the
reunion, John commissioned the noted artist, John Singleton
Copley, to paint portraits of Adams and himself for the Beacon
Hill mansion.

More than two years before, John had finally broken completely with little Sally Jackson. His romantic attentions now
were concentrated almost solely upon Dolly Quincy, and
talk about town had it that he was spending nearly every
evening alone with her. Yet Dolly, always a coquette, was not
one to be captivated easily, despite the pressure Aunt Lydia
constantly brought to bear. Even though John Hancock was
rich and handsome, Dolly thought she might do better.

Despite all his other activities, John still found the time and
energy to concern himself with civic improvements. He had a
bandstand built on the Common for public concerts. He presented a fire engine to the town. He contributed £1,000 toward the building of a new church in Brattle Street, in addition
to giving the church a pulpit, a deacons' seat, a communion
table, and seats for widows and the poor.

In the fall of 1772 the town flew into an uproar again when
it was discovered that the salaries of the judges were to be
paid by the Crown and not by the General Court. A town

meeting was called, with John Hancock as Moderator, to protest this latest move to deprive the people of a part of their
power. The upshot of the meeting was that a new committee
of correspondence was appointed, to consist of twenty-one
members. They were instructed "to state the rights of the
Colonists and of this Province in particular, as men and Chris-
tians and as subjects; and to communicate and publish the
same to the several towns and to the world."

Soon similar committees were appointed by other Massachusetts towns and by other colonies. Alarmed by this activity,
Governor Hutchinson delivered an address to the General
Court on the supremacy of Parliament. His argument was so
forceful that it took all Sam Adams's political shrewdness to
prepare a refutation.

Not long before the elections of May, 1773, which returned
both John Hancock and Sam Adams to the House, a package
of letters fell into the hands of the Liberty Party which gave
Sam Adams the opportunity he had long been seeking: to destroy Thomas Hutchinson and his brother-in-law, Andrew
Oliver. The letters, many of them written years before, contained statements by Hutchinson and Oliver to friends in England urging repressive measures against the colonists. Somehow
or other, Benjamin Franklin had gotten possession of them and
forwarded them to America, with the warning that they were
not to be copied or published.

Hancock, among others, was furious when he read the letters, for Hutchinson had described him with a pen dipped in
acid. The attitude of the colonists had, so the Sons of Liberty
held, been grossly misrepresented. For the time being, however,
they bided their time. Hancock had been one of a group to
accompany Hutchinson to Hartford to attempt settlement of
an ancient border dispute between Massachusetts and New
York; he had difficulty in restraining his anger during the trip.
As soon as he returned, however, he announced to the House

that a horrifying revelation would be made within the next two days.

On a day early in June, the galleries were cleared, and Sam Adams read the letters aloud. Hutchinson and Oliver were not the only ones implicated; there also were letters from Charles Paxton, Judge Auchmuty, and others. When the reading was finished, Hancock made a motion to censure Hutchinson for letters that were intended and designed to overthrow the constitution and introduce arbitrary power into the Province. The motion passed the vote. And, despite Franklin's injunction not to publish the letters, Adams had them printed and distributed, claiming that other copies already were being circulated. The House petitioned King George III to have both Hutchinson and Oliver removed from office.

Having set in motion Hutchinson's political downfall, the Liberty Party now turned its attention to the Tea Act, which had been passed by Parliament in May. By this act the East India Company was allowed to export tea to all places free of duty, including its appointed consignees in America. Since a duty of threepence was kept on all tea imported by colonial merchants other than the East India consignees, the Company could therefore undersell both law-abiding merchants who imported tea from other sources and the colonial smuggler who bought his tea in Holland.

In Boston, as elsewhere in the colonies, the East India Company appointed agents. During the night of November 1 the Sons of Liberty left notices at the door of each of the agents, summoning them to appear beneath the Liberty Tree the following Wednesday to resign their appointments. When none of the consignees appeared at the appointed hour, John Hancock and Sam Adams realized that more forceful action would be necessary.

Toward the end of November the *Dartmouth*, with 114 chests of tea aboard, sailed into Boston Harbor and dropped anchor. A meeting was immediately called; the consignees were forbidden to unload the tea and ordered to ship it back to London immediately. Hutchinson, enraged by the proceedings, looked about for a way to bring a criminal action against the participants, especially Hancock. In a letter to London, he said, "Hancock, notwithstanding, has exposed himself, by his unguarded speeches, more than ever before. . . . It is in everybody's mouth, that Hancock said at the close of the meeting he would be willing to spend his fortune and life itself in so good a cause. But the Secretary says he cannot find anybody who will make an oath to it."

The following week two more ships bearing tea arrived, and John Hancock sent off William Palfrey to acquaint New York and Philadelphia with the proceedings in Boston. The Sons of Liberty placed a guard along the waterfront to see that none of the tea was landed. Despite attempts to send the ships back to England without the duty being paid, Hutchinson gave orders that not one of the ships could leave until the proper sum had been collected.

On December 17 the tea aboard the *Dartmouth* would be liable to seizure for nonpayment of duties. On the sixteenth, several thousand people crowded into Old South Church or stood outside in a steady drizzle of rain. Francis Rotch, owner of the *Dartmouth* and the brother of Hancock's old rival, had been sent to Governor Hutchinson's country home to make one last plea for the ship to be allowed to leave. Meanwhile, one speaker after another harangued the eager multitude in Old South. Many decades later, one eyewitness said that Hancock had been one of the speakers, concluding by declaring, "The matter must be settled before twelve o'clock!" Finally, shortly after twilight, Rotch returned and gave his report: Hutchinson refused to budge from his former position. When Rotch finished speaking, Sam Adams stood up. "This meeting can do nothing more," he shouted, "to save the country!"

It seemed that this was a prearranged signal, for almost immediately a war whoop was heard in the gallery. "Boston Harbor a teapot tonight!" someone roared. Other war whoops were heard outside, and a crowd of several hundred men, most of them disguised as Mohawk Indians, rushed through the cold, moonlit streets toward Griffin's Wharf, where the tea ships were anchored. The horde inside Old South poured out to follow the Indians. As they were leaving, it was claimed that John Hancock's voice could be heard shouting, "Let every man do what is right in his own eyes!"

The *Dartmouth*, *Eleanor*, and *Beaver* were boarded, and within a few hours 342 chests of tea had been broken open and tossed into the salt water of Boston Harbor. When the last chest had been emptied, the Indians and their helpers marched home through the streets, accompanied by fife and drum. Peace descended upon the town.

A rather unreliable witness insisted that he had seen John Hancock down at Griffin's Wharf, wrapped up in a blanket, yet Hancock himself declared that he had not been present. But he made no such claim about his part in planning the Tea Party.

"No one circumstance," he boldly stated to George Haley in London, "could possibly have taken place more effectively to unite the Colonies than this manouvre of the Tea." The Bostonians had expressed their resentment dramatically, and in other colonies their example was followed.

X

The Road to Rebellion

The Committee of Correspondence had discovered an extremely effective way to keep animosity toward the Crown alive in the hearts of the people. Each year, on the anniversary of the Boston Massacre, an elaborate memorial ceremony was held, and an oration delivered by a prominent member of the Liberty Party. On March 5, 1774, John Hancock was scheduled to be the orator.

At ten o'clock in the morning the townspeople assembled in Faneuil Hall. Hancock's drawing power as a speaker had been underestimated. Such a huge crowd turned out that the meeting had to be adjourned to the Old South Church, the largest building in the town of Boston. After a few introductory remarks by Sam Adams, John began to speak.

Even Hancock's staunchest supporters were astounded by his magnetic performance. Graceful, easy, self-possessed, and dignified, he spoke forcefully and dramatically. He knew his audience; he knew how to reach their hearts. Before he had been talking very long, there were, as John Adams noted, many "rainy Eyes."

His sincerity was unmistakable. "Some boast of being friends of government," he said. "I am a friend to righteous government, to a government founded upon the principles of reason and justice; but I glory in publicly avowing my eternal enmity to tyranny; and here suffer me to ask what tenderness, what regard have the rulers of Great Britain manifested in their late transactions, for the security of the persons or property of the inhabitants of these colonies? Or rather, what have they omitted doing to destroy that security?

"They have usurped the right of ruling us, in all cases whatever, by arbitrary laws; they have exercised this pretended right by imposing a tax upon us without our consent; and lest we should show some reluctance at parting with our property, their fleets and armies are sent to enforce their mad and tyrannical pretensions. The town of Boston, ever faithful to the British crown, has been invested by a British fleet; the troops of George the Third have crossed the Atlantic, not to engage an enemy, but to assist a band of traitors in trampling on the rights and liberties of his most loyal subjects; those rights and liberties which, as a father, he ought ever to regard, and as a king, he is bound, in honour, to defend from violation, even at the risk of his own life."

On he spoke, and the more he spoke, the more the emotions of his audience were stirred. He attacked Governor Hutchinson and the courts as mere extensions of the British Parliament; he criticized the policy of the East India Tea Company; he praised the Committee of Correspondence.

"Permit me here to suggest," he said, "a general congress of deputies, from the several houses of assembly on the continent, as the most effectual method of establishing such an union as the present posture of our affairs acquires. At such a congress, a firm foundation may be laid for the security of our rights and liberties; a system may be formed for our common safety, by a strict adherence to which we shall be able to frustrate any attempts to overthrow our constitution; restore peace and harmony to America, and secure honor and wealth to Great Britain."

When John finished speaking, his audience was moved to a frenzy of applause. "This people will never be enslaved with their eyes open," he had said, and the men and women of Boston who heard him were not soon to forget it. Those who had not been present at the Old South were soon told what a spirited performance Hancock had given. Everyone, even Hancock's enemies, agreed that the Liberty Party was fortunate in having so splendid a spokesman.

That night John Adams dined with Justice Quincy and his daughters, among them the Dolly Quincy John Hancock was courting. "The Happiness of the Family where I dined, upon account of [Hancock's] justly applauded Oration, was complete," Adams wrote in his diary. "The Justice and his Daughters were all joyous."

In later years, rumors were circulated that the oration had not actually been written by John Hancock. John Adams said that his cousin Samuel had told him that Benjamin Church and Joseph Warren were the true authors. Others insisted that Sam Adams himself had penned the speech.

The Tories were quick to pick up the gossip. "The first of these chiefs is Adams," wrote one of them, "but, being extremely poor, retails out syllables, sentences, and eulogiums to draw in the multitude. . . . But generous John scorns to let him starve;—far from it;—'t is well known his purse strings have been at Sam's disposal ever since he assisted in making the oration delivered by John, on the 5th of March, 1774, to a crowded audience of Narragansett Indians."

Another Loyalist pamphlet stated, "That mighty wise patriot, Mr. John Hancock, from the Old South Meetinghouse has lately repeated a hash of abusive treasonable stuff, composed for him by the joint efforts of the Rev. Divine

Samuel Cooper, that Rose of Sharon, and the very honest Samuel Adams, Clerk."

If John did not compose the oration, it would not be the first or the last time in history that a public figure had someone else compose his speeches. And it was not the words that spell-bound John's audience so much as the man who delivered them. The wealthiest man in New England had spoken out passionately against tyranny; that was what counted.

John's next public appearance was at the head of the Corps of Independent Cadets, which he had been given command of some time before. The position carried the rank of colonel, a title in which Hancock took unabashed delight. The Corps was to march at the funeral of Andrew Oliver, who had died a few days before Hancock's Massacre Oration, of a broken heart, it was said, over the exposure of his letters to England. Hutchinson was outraged when Hancock offered the services of the Cadets, considering it an affront after Hancock's de-nunciation on the fifth of March. Sam Adams, from other mo-tives, had urged Hancock not to participate. But John, insisting that politics should not follow a man to the grave, led the military company in the procession to the burying ground.

On May 10 Hancock and Sam Adams were again elected Representatives, the same day that news arrived from Eng-land of the passage of the Port Bill. Designed by Parliament to punish the Bostonians, it prohibited the loading or unloading of vessels anywhere in Boston Harbor, and it transferred the seat of government to Salem. The port was to be reopened only when the East India Company had been indemnified for the loss of the tea.

A town meeting was summoned to send forth an appeal to other colonies for sympathy and union, and while the meeting was in session, the frigate *Lively* sailed into Boston Harbor. Aboard was General Thomas Gage, come to supplant Thomas Hutchinson as Governor of Massachusetts.

In the midst of a steady drizzle, Gage landed at Long Wharf. The Independent Cadets, commanded by Colonel John Hancock, were waiting, as ordered, to escort him through town. The parade was awesome. Military companies were drawn up in King Street to salute Gage as he passed; cannon were fired by the batteries; and a splendid banquet was scheduled in Faneuil Hall. But the crowds that assembled in the streets were not impressed.

Gage found the Bostonians as troublesome as Hutchinson had. When the General Court met in Salem, Sam Adams introduced resolutions calling for the appointment of five delegates —James Bowdoin, Thomas Cushing, Robert Treat Paine, and John and Samuel Adams—to meet with delegates from other colonies at a Continental Congress in Philadelphia on September 1.

Before introducing the resolutions, Adams had taken the precaution of having the door locked and ordering the doorkeeper to let no one in and no one out. However, one of the Loyalists managed to sneak out to carry word to Gage of what was afoot. Immediately Gage dispatched the Secretary, Thomas Flucker, to dissolve the meeting, but Flucker was unable to persuade anyone to open the door. Finally he was forced to read the Governor's proclamation to the crowd assembled on the stairs, while the Representatives in the chamber, ignoring his presence outside, passed the resolutions.

Before the summer had progressed very far, Gage and Hancock found themselves at odds. His Excellency, taking offense at what he fancied was a slight by the Corps of Independent Cadets, dismissed Hancock as the group's head. When John informed the Cadets of his dismissal, they voted to return their colors to the Governor and to refuse to serve as his bodyguard in the future. Also, they decided, they would "deliver their Equipage, Musical instruments, &ca. into Colonel Hancock's keeping till some future time, being determin'd not to appear under any other leader while he lives. . . ."

Gage soon discovered that he had done himself more harm than good by quarreling with the idol of the people. Before long the following verse, which appeared in the *Massachusetts Spy*, was being chanted about the streets of Boston:

> Your Colonel H-n-k by neglect
> Has been deficient in respect;
> As he my Sovereign toe ne'er kissed,
> 'Twas proper he should be dismissed;
> I never was, and never will
> By mortal men be treated ill!

Within a few weeks Hancock was to prove himself "deficient" in other respects. Now that Sam Adams and the other delegates had departed for the Continental Congress in Philadelphia, John Hancock was the leading figure in the Liberty Party remaining in Massachusetts. When Gage countermanded the order for the General Court to meet in October, a number of the Representatives gathered on the appointed day and resolved themselves into a Provincial Congress, appointing John Hancock first their chairman and then their president. One of their initial steps was to send a message to Gage attacking the recent acts of Parliament—the so-called "Intolerable Acts" that had closed Boston Harbor to commerce, restricted the power of the town meeting, and ordered a concentration of military forces in Boston. The Provincial Congress, really an illegal body, kept its sessions confidential, moving about from one town to the next, Salem, then Concord, then Cambridge.

The Provincial Congress did more than send messages to Gage. Hancock was appointed head of a Committee of Safety authorized to call out the militia. And before long the Congress began recruiting volunteers, soon to be known as the minutemen.

The First Provincial Congress took one other step. Late in October it issued the proclamation for the annual Thanksgiving, a proclamation always issued in the past by the Royal Governor. The sentiments expressed in the document, which pointedly omitted the customary closing, "God Save the King," were those strongly felt by President Hancock himself: "That God may be pleased to continue to us the blessings we enjoy, and remove the tokens of his displeasure by causing harmony and union to be restored between Great Britain and these colonies, that we may rejoice in the smiles of our sovereign, and in possession of those privileges which have been transmitted to us. . . ."

When Congress adjourned the second week in December, John Hancock hastened back to Boston with a heart that was light and joyous despite the perilous course he had been charting for the past two months. He was eager to see Aunt Lydia again, and he was even more eager to see Aunt Lydia's guest, saucy Dolly Quincy, who had been spending a considerable amount of time in the grand house on Beacon Hill since her mother's death. Aunt Lydia, of course, was delighted to have the two young people together, but if Dolly Quincy shared in the general feeling of joy, she was careful to keep her feelings to herself. Indeed, she made it a point to remark repeatedly to John that the British brigadier general, Hugh, Earl Percy, who drilled his troops on the Common opposite the Hancock mansion, was a very handsome man.

While in Boston, John had a great deal to occupy his mind besides the courtship of Miss Quincy. Smallpox had been brought to town by the British soldiers, and an epidemic was threatening. Nearly every day he had to attend a meeting of the selectmen, who set in motion various measures to control the disease. He also made harried efforts to tend to his business affairs, which were sorely in need of attention.

In February, 1775, the Second Provincial Congress met at

Cambridge, again electing John Hancock president. By now the members of the body had accumulated a considerable list of outrages perpetrated by Gage. The General Court had been dispersed; the Province's powder had been seized; fortifications had been erected on "The Neck" and on the Common; citizens were not allowed to cross the ferry to Charlestown after eight in the evening—on and on the list went.

The Second Provincial Congress assumed the legislative power in Massachusetts, dealing with the Governor as if he were the agent of a foreign nation. Hancock had now committed himself totally to resistance, but actual rebellion was still far from his mind. The temper of the times, however, was sweeping him onward.

While the Second Provincial Congress was holding its initial sessions, decisive steps were being taken in London to enforce obedience in Massachusetts. "I don't wish to alarm you," wrote a Londoner to a friend in America, "but you must not any longer be deceived. Orders have now gone out to take up Mr. Hancock, Adams, Otis, and six of the head men of Boston. I have now a copy of the proceedings before me. My heart aches for Mr. Hancock. Send off expresses immediately that they intend to seize his estate, and have his fine house for General——."

Before this letter reached America, the Second Provincial Congress had adjourned, planning to meet again late in March in Concord. John Hancock and Sam Adams returned to Boston. Even though the town was still overrun with British troops, Sam Adams proceeded with preparations for the annual oration commemorating the Boston Massacre. On March 6 (the fifth was a Sunday), at the Old South Church, Adams and Hancock, together with the Boston selectmen, assembled in the pulpit, which was draped in black. Dr. Joseph Warren was to be the speaker.

Eyewitness accounts differ as to what actually happened,

but all agree that a scheme was afoot to break up the meeting and threaten the three Patriot leaders. One story is that they were to be seized by the redcoats and dragged before General Gage. A British ensign, appointed to give the signal by throwing an egg at Warren, slipped on entering the church and broke the egg. Only for this reason—so the story says—did the plot fail to materialize.

Adams, serving as moderator of the meeting, himself admitted that he expected the British to use the occasion to "beat up a Breeze." When he saw about forty British officers entering the meetinghouse, he ordered the front pews cleared so they would have "no pretence to behave Ill; for it is a good Maxim in Politicks as well as War to put & Keep the Enemy in the wrong." A number of redcoats insisted on sitting on the stairs of the pulpit, and all during Warren's speech they coughed, cleared their throats, or snickered. One of them even tried to frighten Warren by holding out his palm with several bullets on it, but the cool-headed orator simply dropped a handkerchief over the bullets.

Nevertheless, Warren was careful not to refer to the Massacre as "bloody," nor to say anything reflecting on the King or Royal family. When the doctor finished speaking, according to British Lieutenant Barker, John Hancock rose and made a short, inflammatory speech. At this some of the officers shouted, "Fie! Fie!" The crowd, mistaking the shouts for "Fire! Fire!," panicked, fleeing head over heels out through the windows and doors. To make the confusion worse, a regiment of redcoats happened to be marching by Old South just as the crowd tumbled out. At last, order was restored, and the Patriots dispersed, but General Gage issued an order forbidding the parade that had been planned for the evening.

Within two weeks Hancock found himself the center of further disturbances. One evening a number of British officers, carousing through the town, swaggered up Beacon Hill toward the great stone house. Drawing out their swords, they slashed and hacked at the wooden fence. Hancock, incensed, was about to rush out and confront the vandals, but Aunt Lydia urged caution. Any incident involving Hancock might bring out the Boston mob, and a skirmish with the British officers might provoke wholesale bloodshed.

Two nights later, encouraged by the example of their officers, several of the regulars forced their way through the fence and stood about on the front lawn, jeering loudly. Even Aunt Lydia could not restrain her hot-headed nephew. Storming outside, he ordered the rowdy soldiers to leave the premises. They laughed insolently, and their spokesman announced that they had come to see how well his property would do for their barracks. In a short while, they said, his house and stables would be theirs, to do with as they pleased.

Fortunately, Hancock's sense of dignity cooled his temper. Instead of arguing further with the unruly enlisted men, he dispatched a servant to General Gage, with a message protesting the outrage. At this point Gage was willing to do everything he could to maintain order and prevent the sparks of rebellion from bursting forth into a flame. The officer of the guard on the Common was given orders to seize any soldier or officer molesting Colonel Hancock, and the fence was ordered repaired.

By late March Hancock was again in Concord, where the Second Provincial Congress had reassembled. The weather still was bitterly cold, and many of the delegates became more preoccupied with keeping warm than with doing business. Finally a motion was passed stating, "In consideration of the coldness of the season, and that the Congress sit in a room without a fire, *Resolved,* That all those members who incline thereto may sit with their hats on while in Congress."

Much of the talk was concerned with what should be done about calling out the militia, or minutemen, if movements of the British troops warranted such action. The delegates were determined to oppose any further encroachment upon their liberties, yet a number of them, like John Hancock, still thought of themselves as Englishmen only, resisting an oppressive provincial government, but loyal to King George III.

Early in April, with 103 delegates present, the Provincial Congress resolved to call for an armed alliance of Massachusetts, Connecticut, Rhode Island, and New Hampshire. This would be a confederation for their common defense, able to raise and equip a general army. One week later the Congress adjourned, to meet again in May.

John Hancock and Samuel Adams did not plan to be present. By this time they had been designated among the delegates to attend the Second Continental Congress in Philadelphia, scheduled to convene on May 10.

When the session in Concord broke up, both Hancock and Adams decided not to return to Boston. The town was like an armed camp, and the two men suspected that a warrant for their arrest might be issued at any moment. John had another reason for not wanting to return to Beacon Hill. About a week earlier Aunt Lydia, accompanied by Miss Dolly Quincy, had come to stay at the parsonage in Lexington, where John's grandfather had lived, and where his cousin's husband now was the minister. John suggested, and Adams agreed, that it would be sensible to spend the next week or so in Lexington, until the day arrived when they would set out for the Continental Congress in Philadelphia.

So, on April 15, 1775, John Hancock and Samuel Adams rode over to the Clark parsonage in Lexington. Even though cold draughts blew through the carriage, they were relaxed and happy. A pleasant week, they thought, lay ahead.

XI

Shots Ring Out on Lexington Common

While Hancock and Adams were making the short journey
from Concord to Lexington, General Thomas Gage was preparing his troops for a longer expedition. For weeks it had
been whispered about the town that Gage had received two
sets of orders: the first, to seize Hancock and Adams and send
them over to England to be tried as rebels; the second, to hang
them from the town gallows on "The Neck." It was also
widely known that Gage was aware of the military stores being
collected by the Provincial Congress at Concord.

Gage, with 4,000 men under his command and reinforce-
ments on the way, now decided to do something to halt what
was likely to explode at any moment into a civil war. The
stores at Concord were to be destroyed; the rebel leaders
arrested. On April 15, the very day that the Provincial Congress adjourned, the grenadiers and light infantry in Boston
were relieved from duty, supposedly to learn new exercises.
That night the boats belonging to the British transports, recently hauled up and repaired, were launched and moored
beneath the sterns of the men-of-war.

These unusual and highly suspicious movements did not go unnoticed. Silversmith Paul Revere, a favorite messenger of the Boston Committee of Safety, hastened to Dr. Joseph Warren with the news, and Warren ordered him to ride the sixteen miles out to Lexington the following day to warn Hancock and Adams. So on Sunday morning Paul Revere set out.

Reaching Lexington Common, Revere took the right fork, riding a quarter of a mile beyond the meetinghouse to the parsonage, which lay on the west side of the Bedford road. He found a full house. Even with the two-story wing that Thomas Hancock had added at right angles to the old structure, the parsonage consisted of only eight rooms, barely enough space for the Reverend Jonas Clark, his wife Lucy (the sister of Nicholas and William Bowes), and their ten children, Polly, Betsey, Lucy, Liddy, Patty, Sally, Thomas, Jonas, William, and Peter, ranging in age from sixteen years to five months. Hancock and Adams had been given one of the bedrooms in the new wing; Aunt Lydia and Dolly Quincy the other. Hancock had also brought along his clerk, John Lowell, and a large trunk especially designed to fit behind the chaise in which they would be traveling to Philadelphia; but there was simply no room at the parsonage for clerk and trunk. They had been deposited at Buckman's Tavern, just across the road from the meetinghouse.

Neither Hancock nor Adams set much store by the warning that their lives were in danger, but they were concerned for the supplies at Concord. As chairman of the Committee of Safety, Hancock dispatched an express ordering that the arms and munitions be scattered in various hiding places. Riders were also sent out to the neighboring villages to give the alert. Mischief was afoot, and the minutemen made ready.

On Tuesday, April 18, General Gage prepared to move, confident that his plans had been kept secret. To Lieutenant Colonel Smith and Major Pitcairn he gave sealed orders. Sev-

eral parties of officers were stationed on roads leading out of
Boston to keep news of the expedition from reaching the countryside. Nevertheless, two warnings from members of the
Committee of Safety got through to Hancock in the early evening. Seated in the small study off the kitchen, John penned a
swift reply to one of the messages. "I am much obliged for
your notice," he wrote. "I intend doing myself the pleasure
of being with you to-morrow." But the morrow would find
him fleeing for his life.

Shortly before ten o'clock that night British soldiers were
observed marching toward the beach at the bottom of the
Common. The moment word of the imminent embarkation
reached Joseph Warren, he dispatched Paul Revere and another Son of Liberty, William Dawes, by separate routes to
put Hancock and Adams on guard. Dawes slipped out of town
by way of "The Neck"; Revere rowed across to Charlestown,
borrowed John Larkin's horse, and set out on the moonlit
road that would lead him to Medford, Menotomy, Lexington,
and on into immortality.

Meanwhile, one of the parties of British officers rode into
Lexington and took the left fork toward Concord. Certain
that the British were not on a pleasure trip, the minutemen
began to gather at Buckman's Tavern, and Sergeant William
Munroe took eight men to guard the distinguished visitors at
the Clark parsonage. Crowded as the house was, it was comfortable, and John Hancock was too happy at being with
Dolly again to consider moving to newer—and safer—quarters.
Sam Adams had other reasons for wanting to stay. Properly
managed, a stand by the minutemen against the advancing British troops might unleash the storm of rebellion that had been
brewing for almost a decade. So, while the redcoats marched
along the country roads, the Reverend Jonas Clark, Lucy
Clark, the ten little Clarks, John Hancock, Sam Adams, Aunt
Lydia, and pert Dolly Quincy all retired to their beds. But

before retiring they requested, Sergeant Munroe reported, "that they might not be disturbed by any noise about the house." Although William Munroe did his best, none of them had a very quiet night.

Shortly before midnight, with a clatter of hooves, John Larkin's horse galloped up to the parsonage, husky Paul Revere astride his back. Dismounting, Revere strode toward the house, to find Munroe barring his way. Wasting no time on introductions, Revere loudly demanded admittance. When Munroe hushed him, the bluff silversmith from Boston nearly exploded. "Noise!" Revere shouted. "You'll have noise enough before long. The regulars are coming out."

Munroe let him pass. Revere pounded at the door. Up flew a window, out of which Jonas Clark thrust his huge head with its bulldog jaw. What was all this racket, he wanted to know. Who was this stranger, and what did he want? By this time Hancock had recognized his friend's voice. "Come in, Revere," he called. "We're not afraid of *you*."

Revere told them his errand and delivered the message from Dr. Warren. The King's troops were out, he reported, supposedly a brigade of twelve or fifteen hundred. They had gone over to Lechmere's Point in Cambridge and were by now well on the way to Lexington and Concord. Within a half hour William Dawes rode up with a duplicate message from Warren.

Within the parsonage all was now commotion. Aunt Lydia, Dolly Quincy, and the Clark children were awake. Everyone was talking at once. Hancock sent one of the sentries running down to Lexington Common to give the alarm. Soon the bell in the meetinghouse was ringing, and the militia began to assemble. Couriers were sent out toward Cambridge to gather additional information.

By two o'clock in the morning 130 armed men had assembled under Captain John Parker. Loading their guns with pow-

der and ball, they waited in the chilly night air for the redcoats
to appear. As time passed and no troops came in sight, Captain
Parker finally dismissed his men, ordering them to muster again
at the beat of the drum. Those who lived near the Common
went home. The rest gathered in Buckman's Tavern.

Revere and Dawes, after refreshing themselves and their
horses, had departed for Concord, and John Hancock pulled
out his sword and gun and began cleaning them. He was determined, as Dolly Quincy said, "to go out to the plain by the
meetinghouse, where the battle was, to fight with the men who
had collected."

Dolly's private opinion was that the minutemen were rather
a sorry lot. They were, she said, "but partially provided with
arms, and those they had were in most miserable order." Less
than two weeks before, while she and Aunt Lydia were still
in the Beacon Hill mansion, Dolly had watched the splendidly
dressed British troops drilling on Boston Common under the
command of Hugh, Earl Percy. Just as Lexington Common,
with its two acres, was a paltry spot (so Dolly probably
thought) compared to the rolling expanse of Boston Common,
so the Lexington farmers made a poor showing in contrast to
the well-trained ranks of scarlet-coated Britishers.

In the parsonage kitchen a heated argument had started;
it would last until dawn. On one side were Jonas Clark and
Sam Adams; on the other, John Hancock. Overcome with the
excitement of the moment, John had let his love for the dramatic get the better of him. He was convinced that his place
lay with the farmers on the Common, and little that Clark or
Adams had to say could dissuade him. Hot-headed and impetuous, he was spoiling for a fight, and the fact that the fight
would be with the soldiers of his King made little difference.

Although there seems to be strong evidence that Sam Adams
was busily urging Captain John Parker and his minutemen
to make a stand against the redcoats, he was strongly opposed

to having Hancock join the fighters. Hancock, Adams felt, had a more important role to play than as a sharpshooter in a minor skirmish. Finally he clapped John on the shoulder, saying, "That is not our business. We belong to the cabinet."

At four o'clock in the morning the argument was still raging when Paul Revere again burst into the house. He and Dawes had been seized by a party of British officers on the road to Concord, but he managed to escape, making his way across the burying ground and some pastures to the parsonage. Adams and Hancock would endanger their lives by remaining any longer, he said; flight was imperative. Before leaving, John insisted on going down to the Common to talk with the minutemen. On returning to the house he again stated his reluctance to leave the battle behind him. He was also reluctant to leave Dolly, who was to stay at the parsonage with Aunt Lydia. At last, however, he gave way, and Adams, Revere, and John Lowell bundled him out the door to the waiting chaise. "If I had my musket," he protested, "I would never turn my back on these troops."

No sooner had the party concealed itself in a clump of trees about two miles north of Lexington than John remembered his trunk. Full of important—and probably incriminating— papers belonging to the Provincial Congress, it had been left behind in Lowell's room in Buckman's Tavern, an easy prize for the British. Lowell and Revere were sent back to carry it to a place of safety, while Hancock and Adams drove on to the home of Widow Jones in Woburn. Dawn was breaking as they passed through the fields, and Sam Adams felt his heart swell with an almost uncontrollable joy, for to him this was the dawn of American independence, a moment toward which he had directed all his energies for more than a decade. "O! what a glorious morning is this!" he exclaimed, and, for him, it was the most glorious morning of his life.

Back in Lexington, Captain Parker had ordered the drum

to beat at half past four; the redcoats were reported to be less than a mile-and-a-half from town. From Buckman's Tavern and from the houses near the Common, the militia began to reassemble, some fifty to seventy men in all. By now Revere and Lowell had reached the chamber where Hancock's trunk had been left.

"While we were getting the trunk," said Paul Revere, "we saw the British very near, upon a full march. We hurried towards Mr. Clark's house. In our way, we passed through the militia. . . . When we had got about one hundred yards from the meeting-house, the British troops appeared on both sides of the meeting-house. In their front was an officer on horseback. They made a short halt; when I saw, and heard, a gun fired, which appeared to be a pistol. Then I could distinguish two guns, and then a continual roar. . . ." Neither Revere nor Lowell stayed to see more. Their task was to get John Hancock's trunk to the parsonage, and toward the parsonage they went.

No one was ever quite sure who had fired the first shot. Captain Parker had ordered the militia to disperse and not to fire. Major Pitcairn had commanded the redcoats to surround the rebels and disarm them, but he, too, told his men not to fire. However, as that first shot rang out, echoing across Lexington Common, the British troops broke ranks and began shooting at will. When the smoke cleared away, eight of the minutemen lay dead, and ten lay wounded.

Aunt Lydia herself came close to being one of the casualties. As the redcoats were approaching the Common, she had opened the parsonage door and peered down the road, curious to see what was going on. One of the first British bullets whizzed right by her head and struck the barn.

"What is that?" she cried out.

When the Clarks told her that it was a bullet, even fearless Aunt Lydia must have trembled a bit. Dolly Quincy had chosen a safer vantage point, one of the bedchamber windows, from which she watched the brief skirmish from beginning to end.

After the battle, two of the wounded men were carried to the parsonage. Dolly was no more sympathetic toward the minutemen now than she had been earlier in the morning. "One of them," she said, "whose head was grazed by a ball, insisted on it that he was dead." He was, she added, "more scared than hurt." The other man had been shot in the arm. Dolly admitted that he behaved better than the first.

By now Dolly and Aunt Lydia both had their cloaks and bonnets on and were adding their bit to the tumult that reigned in the Clark household. While Aunt Lydia helped Lucy Clark dress the smaller children, Dolly rushed about with Jonas, hiding money, watches, and other valuables in every conceivably safe place from the potato bin to the garret.

Not long after the redcoats had marched out of Lexington on the road toward Concord, a messenger from Hancock arrived at the Clark parsonage. Dolly and Aunt Lydia were to join Sam Adams and John at the Widow Jones's house in Woburn, and they were to bring along the handsome salmon that had been sent to them for dinner. A carriage was brought round to the door, and in a short while the two women and the salmon were reunited with the men General Gage considered the most dangerous of the rebels. By now the British troops under Colonel Smith and Major Pitcairn had reached Concord, and a small detachment was moving on toward Concord's North Bridge, where the minutemen lay waiting.

While the "shot heard round the world" was being fired at the North Bridge, Sam Adams, John Hancock, Aunt Lydia, and Dolly Quincy sat in the kitchen of Widow Jones's house, watching the salmon being prepared for their noon meal. Even to Miss Dolly's fastidious taste, it was "nicely cooked." Just as the group was about to sit down at the table, a man from

Lexington burst into the house. His home was on the main road between Concord and Lexington, down which the redcoats were now retreating, running a gauntlet of fire from farmhouse windows and behind stone walls and barns.

"The British are coming! The British are coming!" he shouted, half petrified by fear. "My wife's in etarnity now!"

Hancock and Adams did not wait to hear more. Leaving the tasty salmon on Widow Jones's table, they fled to a neighboring swamp, where they remained concealed until the alarm was over. Aunt Lydia and Dolly stayed behind in the house. In 1775 women and children were not considered fair targets in warfare. And Aunt Lydia's ferocious scowl and Miss Dolly's cool stare would have made even the most unruly British grenadier think twice about disturbing them.

When the two men returned to the house, they paused only long enough for John and Dolly to have a lovers' quarrel. Dolly announced that she was returning to Boston the next day. Her father was there, and she was worried about his safety.

John was now taking a more realistic view of affairs than he had a few hours earlier, when he wanted to rush out and fight on Lexington Common. "No, madam," he said. "You shall not return so long as there is a British bayonet left in Boston."

Dolly's eyes flashed. "Recollect, Mr. Hancock," she said, "I am not under your control yet. I *shall* go in to my father tomorrow." She meant every word she said. Years later she was to confide to a friend, "At that time I should have been very glad to have got rid of him."

But Aunt Lydia had a stronger will than pretty Dolly Quincy. She would not let Dolly go back to Boston, and she would not let her get rid of John Hancock. Indeed, Aunt Lydia seems to have made up her mind not to let Dolly out of her sight until Miss Quincy became Mrs. Hancock.

Fearing that the British would now be after them with a vengeance, Hancock and Adams decided to take refuge farther from Lexington. One of Widow Jones's domestics conducted them through the woods to the home of Amos Wyman in the town of Billerica, where they were served a dinner of brown bread, cold pork, and cold potatoes. What became of the tasty salmon history does not record.

It was after dark before the bedraggled redcoats stumbled back into Charlestown and set up camp. All along the route toward Boston they had been harassed by snipers, and there was little they could do except burn a few houses and barns along the way. It seemed that the whole countryside had turned out to oppose them.

Reports of the day's action drifted back to Sam Adams and John Hancock in Billerica. As they went to bed that night, Sam Adams felt certain that the farmers and tradesmen who had fought along the country roads were no longer men fighting for their rights as Englishmen; they were now Americans. As for Hancock and himself, they were irrevocably committed to leading a rebellion.

Unlike his companion, John Hancock did not regard this as the first day of American independence. He prayed that—despite the blood shed during the fighting—wounds might be healed. Even though a civil war was under way, reconciliation with the mother country might still be possible if the rights of the colonists were restored.

XII

☆ ☆ ☆
☆

"Our Country Must Be Saved"

John Hancock, Sam Adams, and Hancock's large trunk rolled into the town of Worcester on April 24, where they expected to meet the other Massachusetts delegates to the Second Continental Congress at Philadelphia. Instead, they were joined by Aunt Lydia and Dolly, who had been traveling through the Province by a different route.

Soon after arriving, John dashed off a letter to the Committee of Safety at the Provincial Congress, already in session at Watertown. "I beg, by the return of this express," he wrote, "to hear from you, and pray, furnish us with depositions of the conduct of the troops, the certainty of their firing first, and every circumstance relative to the conduct of the troops from the 19th instant, to this time, that we may be able to give some account of matters as we proceed, especially at Philadelphia."

Not only did John want to justify the actions of the minutemen; he wanted to be sure that their fervor was kept high. "Are our men in good spirits?" he asked. "For God's sake do not suffer the spirit to subside, until they have perfected the

120

reduction of our enemies. Boston *must* be entered; the troops
must be sent away, . . . Our friends are valuable, but our country must be saved."

The failure of the other delegates to appear worried him.
"Where is Mr. Cushing. Are Mr. Paine and Mr. John Adams
to be with us? What are we to depend upon? We travel rather
as deserters, which I will not submit to."

Not joining the skirmish at Lexington still bothered him,
and now—now he was on the way to Philadelphia while Massachusetts seethed with trouble. By this time, less than a week
after Lexington and Concord, there was little indication
whether the action taken by the minutemen would be supported by the other colonies. Perhaps Massachusetts would
have to stand alone against the wrath of King George III. If so,
John wanted to be in Massachusetts, not far away in Philadelphia. His heart spoke when he wrote, "We travel rather as
deserters."

But Sam Adams was with him, and Sam's will was strong.
Now that Massachusetts had taken the first step toward independence, Adams felt it imperative that the other colonies
be pushed to take similar steps. The Second Continental Congress offered a vantage point from which further rebellion
could be incited. Let Massachusetts take care of herself, Sam
urged; he and John should move on.

On April 27 they did move on, together with Aunt Lydia
and Dolly, to Hartford. There, two days later, Adams and
Hancock held a secret meeting with Governor Jonathan Trumbull and the Connecticut Council of Safety. The purpose of
the meeting was to discuss an attack on Fort Ticonderoga,
a strategy that Adams and Dr. Warren had explored earlier.
Adams felt that one of the first objectives of the British would
be to split the colonies. A British army sent from Ticonderoga
on Lake Champlain down the Hudson to Manhattan Island
could separate New England from the South. However, if the

colonists captured Ticonderoga, the King's troops would have
to resort to other tactics. Fortune smiled upon the rebels. Ten
days after the meeting at Hartford, Fort Ticonderoga fell to
a colonial force under Ethan Allen and Benedict Arnold.

From Hartford the four travelers moved down to Fairfield
on Long Island Sound. To John's great sorrow (and probably
to Sam Adams's equally great relief), Aunt Lydia and Dolly
decided not to continue to Philadelphia. They would be welcome guests at the mansion of Thomas Hancock's old friend,
Thaddeus Burr, high sheriff of Fairfield County. Standing just
a short distance from the courthouse, church, and jail, the
Burr residence was one of the finest homes in Connecticut.
Three years later it was to be left a heap of smoldering ashes
by marauding British troops, but neither Dolly nor Aunt
Lydia would be present to watch the devastation.

Just before three o'clock on the first Saturday afternoon in
May, thoroughly fatigued after more than two weeks of
traveling, John Hancock in his carriage, with Sam Adams be-
side him, rolled into King's Bridge, just north of the town of
New York. Here they finally met up with the other Massachu-
setts delegates, Thomas Cushing, John Adams, and Robert
Treat Paine, as well as the Connecticut delegates, Silas Deane,
Roger Sherman, and Eliphalet Dyer.

After dinner the procession set out for New York, John
Hancock's carriage leading all the rest. Word of their approach
preceded them, and three miles from the city they were met
by a cheering throng. There were, John wrote to Dolly, "the
Grenadier Company and Regiment of the City Militia under
Arms, Gentlemen in Carriages and on Horseback, and many
Thousands of Persons on Foot, the Roads fill'd with people,
and the greatest Cloud of Dust I ever saw."

About a mile from town several men in the jubilant crowd
noticed how fatigued Hancock's horses were, after the hectic
pilgrimage from Lexington. They attempted to unharness the

horses in order to drag the carriages of the delegates by hand. Hancock protested against this sort of homage; and because Silas Deane's horses could not be managed amid the crowd, smoke, and noise, the attempt was abandoned for the moment.

"When I got to the Entrance of the City," John told Dolly, "and the Numbers of Spectators increas'd to perhaps Seven Thousand or more, they Declar'd they would have the Horses out and would Drag me themselves thro' the City." Once again, although flattered, John objected vigorously.

After several salutes were fired by the battalion, the procession paraded through town to the corner of Wall Street, then down Broadway and on to Fraunces' Tavern. "The doors, the windows, the stoops, the roofs of the piazzas," Silas Deane informed his wife, "were loaded with all ranks, ages and sexes; in short, I feared every moment lest someone would be crushed to death." Once the delegates had entered Fraunces' Tavern, the crowd gave three huzzas and then slowly dispersed.

To John and the other Massachusetts delegates, the demonstration had been extremely heartening. The town of New York was known as a hotbed of Loyalists, and if this much support could be mustered for the step taken by Massachusetts, what would the reception be in the other colonies?

By the time John entered Fraunces' Tavern he was exhausted, and his face and eyes were swollen with sunburn. But he was not yet to be allowed to rest. One after another, many of New York's leading citizens called to pay their respects to the various delegates, and it was ten o'clock before the group sat down to a supper of fried oysters. At eleven, he strolled to his lodgings a few doors away. That night he slept soundly, despite the guard of grenadiers in blue and scarlet uniforms set at the door, and despite the fact that the place where he lodged was the King's Inn.

On Sunday he rose at five o'clock, attended church both in

the morning and the afternoon, and spent most of the evening writing a letter to "my dear Dolly," telling her in detail everything that had happened since their parting in Fairfield. "I Beg you will write me," he pleaded; "do acquaint me every Circumstance Relative to that Dear Aunt of Mine; write Lengthy and often. . . . Is your Father out [of Boston]? As soon as you know, do acquaint me, and send me the Letters, and I will then write him. Pray let me hear from you by every Post. God Bless you my D' Girl, and believe me most Sincerely, Yours most Affectionately. . . ." As it turned out, John was a much more frequent—and ardent—letter writer than Dolly. Miss Quincy found that Fairfield offered a lively social whirl, and when John was out of sight, she turned her eyes elsewhere.

Leaving New York early Monday morning, the delegates crossed by ferry to the Jersey shore, then proceeded through Elizabeth to Woodbridge, where, Silas Deane reported, "all were in arms—though these were very rough troops, and afforded us some diversion; but they meant well." That night they lodged beyond New Brunswick, and on Tuesday traveled to Princeton, where the president and students of the college received them. After dinner at Trenton, they rode on to Bristol, and, after a short night's sleep, set out for Philadelphia early Wednesday.

About six miles from the city two hundred men on horseback, with swords drawn, were waiting to escort them. First among the delegates rode John Hancock and Sam Adams. "At about two miles distance," Silas Deane wrote, "we were met by a company, on foot, and then by a Company of Riflemen in their uniform, which is very curious. Thus rolling and gathering like a snowball we approached the City, which was full of people, and the crowd as great as at New York; the bells all ringing, and the air rent with shouts and huzzas . . . and after much fatigue we were landed at the New City Tavern. Happily a rain had laid the dust, and we were not so troubled as at New York."

Delegates from many of the other colonies had reached Philadelphia before the contingent from Massachusetts, Connecticut, and New York. On May 5, Christopher Marshall, a prominent Philadelphia businessman, had noted in his diary the arrival from London of the *Pennsylvania Packet*, "in which came passenger, Dr. Benjamin Franklin, to the satisfaction of his friends and the lovers of liberty." The next day two New Hampshire delegates were in town. May 9 brought representatives from Delaware, Maryland, North and South Carolina, as well as those from Virginia, including Peyton Randolph, George Washington, Patrick Henry, Richard Henry Lee, and Benjamin Harrison.

According to another Philadelphian, a Loyalist, the reception accorded the radicals from New England did not sit well with the moderates from the Middle and Southern colonies. Speaking of the procession into town, the Loyalist noted, "Every mark of respect that could be, was expressed:—not much I presume to the secret liking of their fellow delegates from the other colonies, who doubtless had to digest the distinction as easily as they could."

The two Adamses had encountered the same antagonism in the First Continental Congress, and many of the same men still were represented. For all his skill as a politician, and for all his experience as a mob manipulator in Boston, Sam Adams found that the Continental Congress offered a challenge he could not easily meet. Too many men were distrustful of the extremes to which he might go. The wealthy, cosmopolitan John Hancock, on the other hand, was a man much to the liking of the landed aristocrats from New York and the plantation owners from the South. His presence among the Massachusetts delegation helped to remove some of the suspicions held toward the two Adamses.

It was nearly one o'clock before the New Englanders reached the City Tavern, the town's most elegant hostelry, at the corner of Second and Walnut Streets. The opening session of the Second Continental Congress was about to begin, and John Hancock hastened to make ready to attend.

In less than a month, he realized, events had carried him a long way down the road of rebellion. The British troops in Boston were bottled up, besieged by an armed camp of farmers and tradesmen who had hastily responded to the alarm raised by the skirmishes at Lexington and Concord. English officers now lived in the Hancock mansion on Beacon Hill. His ships and shops had undoubtedly been seized. He and Sam Adams were marked men. Despite the bright sun shining on the Philadephia streets, dark clouds of uncertainty were gathering.

XIII

The Second Continental Congress

On the day that Fort Ticonderoga fell to Ethan Allen and Benedict Arnold, the Second Continental Congress convened in Pennsylvania's State House on Chestnut Street, just a few blocks from the City Tavern. With 40,000 people, Philadelphia was now the largest city in the colonies, and a city of sharp contrasts. Society was dominated by a conservative aristocracy, openly hostile to men such as Sam Adams. Yet the inns, taverns, coffeehouses, and cobbled streets were filled with a throng of backwoodsmen, Swedes, Dutch, Indians, all of them jostling each other and the Quakers. It was a beautiful city, obviously prosperous, with rows of handsome brick houses set along parallel streets bisected by parallel cross streets, equally wide and straight, named, as John Adams noted, "from forest and fruit trees—Pear Street, Apple Street, Walnut Street, Chestnut Street."

The State House, where the Continental Congress met, was one of the most gracious buildings in the city. The Pennsylvania Assembly had given permission for the forty-eight delegates to Congress to use a spacious, white-paneled room on the ground floor at the east end, with tall windows lining two sides.

It seemed to John Hancock that everywhere he went he saw and heard military companies at drill, in the State House yard, in the Factory yard, and in a field two-miles square, west of the city. At least thirty companies were under arms, including a group of young Quakers. "Such is the spirit and alacrity" of the Quakers, Christopher Marshall observed, "that few, if any, of the companies will sooner learn the military art and discipline, and make a handsomer appearance, nor be more ready to assert, at the risk of their lives, the freedom of America on Constitutional principles."

Once the Continental Congress had convened, it elected Peyton Randolph of Virginia its President, and Charles Thomson, known as the Sam Adams of Philadelphia, its Secretary. The Congress got down to business immediately, but not the sort of business its more ardent members had hoped for. Not much was said about adopting the rebel army outside Boston; even less was said about independence. Most of the forty-eight men present had no authority from their colonies to do any more than attend the sessions and discuss the various difficulties they were having with England.

Several days were spent in reading aloud depositions taken from eyewitnesses at Lexington and Concord; a petition was prepared, to be sent to England, attempting to prove that the redcoats, not the minutemen, had fired the first shots. Then Congress considered "ways and means to supply the Colonies with ammunition and military stores" and "the best means for establishing post for conveying letters and intelligence through the continent." Then, much to Sam Adams's chagrin, it was resolved that no expedition should be undertaken against Canada.

John Hancock's popularity among the people was spreading. "King Hancock" they called him, and they meant it as the highest praise. Of all the members of the Continental Congress,

Hancock, by far, cut the most dashing figure (even though Colonel Washington was there in the buff and blue uniform of the Virginia militia). He also attracted the most abuse from the Loyalists. Soon after his arrival in Philadelphia, Tories were chanting:

> Yankee Doodle came to town
> For to buy a firelock;
> We will tar and feather him,
> And so we will John Hancock.

Two weeks after Congress convened, Peyton Randolph decided to return to Virginia to accept the speakership of the General Assembly. Hancock, having proved his ability as a presiding officer at the Boston town meetings and at the Massachusetts Provincial Congress, was unanimously elected to succeed Randolph as President of Congress. The task that faced him was monumental. Not only was the Continental Congress an illegal body, it was a body of men with amazingly divergent views toward England and toward each other, a body with little organization, no credit, and no authority to borrow money or levy taxes. Moreover, the group was riddled with distrust of the Massachusetts delegation, at least the part of it composed of the two Adamses.

At one end of the white-paneled room in which the Congress held its meetings stood the President's table and chair. Benjamin Harrison escorted Hancock across the room to the chair, fully aware, as were the other delegates, that the man he walked beside was regarded as an arch-rebel by the Crown. As a gesture of defiance to Great Britain, Hancock's election was a dramatic move.

Meanwhile, John was having troubles with his dear Dolly. Less than two weeks after John's departure from Fairfield, Thaddeus Burr's nineteen-year-old nephew came to pay a visit. Aaron Burr was clever and good-looking, and Dolly found his company delightful. The only problem, she admitted years later, was that Aunt Lydia would not leave them alone together for a moment. Aunt Lydia was a wise woman. Not only did she want to protect John's interests, she also wanted to keep Dolly from making a fool of herself. Miss Dolly had just passed her twenty-eighth birthday, and Aaron Burr was nine years her junior.

Even if rumors of Dolly's defection did not reach John's ears, he knew that something was wrong. He had written a number of letters. He had sent presents—an umbrella, a fan, stockings, two caps, a "very pretty light Hat," and a "neat Airy Summer Cloak." Not a word of thanks, not a word about anything, was heard from his fickle fiancée. The gifts, incidentally, were carried to Fairfield by Dr. Benjamin Church of Boston, who had been an active member of the Liberty Party since its founding. Within a few months Dr. Church was to be unmasked as a traitor, a scandal that would shock the colonies from Massachusetts to Georgia.

On June 10 John ventured to send Dolly a note of protest. "I am almost prevail'd on to think," he wrote, "that my letters to my Aunt & you are not read, for I cannot obtain a reply, I have ask'd million questions & not an answer to one. . . . I really Take it extreme unkind, pray my D^r use not so much Ceremony & Reservedness, why can't you use freedom in writing, be not afraid of me. . . . I Beg, my Dear Dolly, you will write me often & long Letters, I will forgive the past if you will mend in future. Do ask my Aunt to make me up & send me a Watch String, & do you make up another & send me, I wear them out fast. I want some little thing of your doing."

Dolly's answer, if any, has not been preserved.

Fortunately, John did not have a great deal of time to brood upon Dolly's neglect. As President of Congress, he was called upon to be diplomat, mediator, and, in his spare moments, correspondence clerk. The radicals were pressing for independence; the moderates insisted on negotiating with England for a redress of wrongs. John's task was to keep the two factions together as a unified body.

The problem of a commander-in-chief for the army gathered outside Boston still faced Congress. If it appointed a commanding general, then the army would become the Continental Army, and Congress would be responsible for its actions. Even the Massachusetts delegates disagreed among themselves as to what should be done. Sam Adams tended to feel that the soldiers should elect their own commander. Cushing argued that, since most of the soldiers were New Englanders, their general should be a New England man. Robert Paine thought that the honor should go to his old friend, Artemas Ward, who was already serving with the troops. Hancock, so John Adams thought, wanted the honor for himself. And John Adams had set his heart on the tall Virginian, George Washington.

Before presenting the matter for debate in Congress, the younger Adams set out to win support for his candidate by approaching delegates outside the walls of the State House. Throughout, he was careful not to let a word of his plans reach the ears of his friend, Hancock.

Just before the hour Congress was to meet on June 14, John Adams took his cousin Sam into his confidence as they strolled about the State House yard. That very morning, he said, he planned to present a motion that the Continental Congress adopt the army and appoint Colonel Washington its commander. The two men went inside, and as soon as the session convened, John Adams rose to speak.

Sitting at the table facing the room, John Hancock had no inkling of what was coming. According to John Adams, Hancock's face wore a pleased look while the army at Cambridge was being discussed, but when Washington was nominated, the Boston merchant seemed resentful and chagrined. Then

Sam Adams rose to second the nomination, and Hancock showed more resentment.

No one except John Adams seemed to notice this reaction in Hancock. In view of Hancock's generosity to both the Adamses, it is possible that the younger cousin, suffering from a guilty conscience at having maneuvered behind Hancock's back, imagined—or exaggerated—his reaction. Hancock, often charged by his enemies with vanity and conceit, may indeed have wanted the privilege of declining the appointment; he may even have wanted the position itself. But it seems more likely that his resentment—if he was resentful—was caused by the guile and secrecy with which John and Sam Adams had acted. Hancock never gave either man his wholehearted trust again.

Adams's proposal was not greeted with immediate enthusiasm. Cushing and Robert Paine expressed disagreement. So did Sherman of Connecticut and Pendleton of Virginia, a member of the same delegation as Washington. Some delegates were in favor of General Ward, others in favor of General Charles Lee, still others in favor of Hancock himself. After considerable debate, the session closed without any action being taken.

That evening, and late into the night, John Adams campaigned for Washington. A very persuasive man when he wanted to be, he finally convinced Washington's opponents to abandon their opposition. The next morning Washington was nominated again and unanimously elected. The following day, as President of Congress, Hancock proffered the appointment, which Washington, not without misgivings, accepted. It was an awesome responsibility.

While the Continental Congress debated about the army outside Boston, events in Boston were moving toward a crisis. On June 12 General Thomas Gage issued a proclamation declaring martial law. To spare further bloodshed, he announced, "I do hereby in his Majesty's name offer and promise, his most gracious pardon to all persons who shall forthwith lay down their arms and return to the duties of peaceable subjects."

Two men, and two men only, were excluded from this general pardon, Samuel Adams and John Hancock, "whose offenses," Gage said, "are of too flagitious a nature to admit of any other consideration than that of condign punishment."

Even in England Gage's statement was regarded with a certain amount of skepticism, and in America the patriot press greeted it with jeers. The *New England Chronicle* reprinted the proclamation with the following note:

> As it is replete with consummate impudence, the most abominable lies, and stuffed with daring expressions of tyranny, as well as rebellion against the established constitutional authority, both of Great Britain and of the American States, no one will hesitate in pronouncing it to be the *genuine* production of that perfidious tyrant, Thomas Gage.

The *Boston Gazette* ridiculed the entire proclamation in a long satirical poem, of which one verse ran:

> But then I must out of this plan lock
> Both Samuel Adams and John Hancock,
> For those vile traitors (like bedentures)
> Must be tucked up at all adventures,
> As any proffer of a pardon
> Would only tend those rogues to harden.

No sooner had Washington departed for Cambridge than a dusty courier rode into Philadelphia, bearing news from Massachusetts even more startling than Gage's proclamation. After nightfall on June 16 more than a thousand American troops had moved onto Charlestown peninsula to construct a redoubt on Breed's Hill. The following day they were attacked by redcoats under the command of General William Howe. Charlestown went up in flames. Driven first from Breed's Hill, then from Bunker Hill, the patriots finally retreated from the peninsula, fighting fiercely for every yard of ground.

Neither side took much pride in the day's work. The British suffered well over a thousand casualties, many of them officers. Although the Americans lost only about four hundred killed or wounded, General Artemas Ward and his staff had proved themselves woefully inadequate in the face of emergency. John Hancock and the other members of the Continental Congress took heart in the knowledge that Washington was on the way to take charge as Commander-in-Chief.

On June 18, the news of the battle not yet having reached him, John Hancock wrote to inform Dr. Joseph Warren of Washington's appointment. "He is a Gentleman you will all like," he noted. What Hancock did not know was that Dr. Warren had fallen the day before, shot through the head as he fought with the patriots at Breed's Hill.

Congress was now spurred on to action. In July the so-called "Olive Branch Petition" was sent to King George III, pledging loyalty and requesting that hostile actions cease until a reconciliation could be negotiated. Later that month the delegates passed another important resolution, the "Declaration of the Causes and Necessities of Taking Up Arms," in which they expressed their determination to die rather than be enslaved.

John Hancock's urge to take up arms against the British troops now asserted itself. On July 10, 1775, he wrote to Washington, "I must beg the favor that you will reserve some berth for me, in such department as you may judge most proper; for I am determined to act under you, if it be to take a firelock and join the ranks as volunteer." The request placed Washington in a difficult position, for Hancock was too popular a figure and too powerful a politician to offend. His reply, couched in very diplomatic terms, was that he had very little to offer "equal to Colonel Hancock's Merits and worthy of his Acceptance." Colonel Hancock did not pursue the matter further.

By early August the delegates were impatient to be off to their homes, where the pressure of personal affairs demanded their attention. It was voted to adjourn until the first week in September, and Hancock and the two Adamses set off for Massachusetts. Hancock planned to make a brief visit to Cambridge, then hurry back to Fairfield, where, he hoped, Miss Dolly Quincy might at last consent to marry him.

A trip to Massachusetts had its dangers. If either Hancock or Sam Adams fell into the hands of Gage's troops, they might well end up dangling from the Boston town gallows as a warning to other rebels. And both men knew the popular Tory ballad that promised them a similar fate:

> As for their King, that John Hancock,
>   And Adams, if they're taken;
> Their heads for signs shall hang up high
>   Upon the hill called Beacon!

XIV

☆ ☆ ☆

☆

The Road to Independence

Having braved the perils of a visit to Cambridge and come through unscathed, John Hancock rode back into Philadelphia in early September with a far more attractive companion than Sam Adams. Beside him in the handsome carriage sat his new bride. After years of hesitation, Dolly had finally decided to accept John's proposal, and Aunt Lydia gave her little opportunity to change her mind. August 28, 1775, was set for the ceremony, and on August 28 the wedding took place. Dolly must have been a bit disappointed by the modesty of the occasion. Compared to Boston and the mansion on Beacon Hill, Fairfield and the Burr residence had little splendor—at least to Dolly's sophisticated eyes—and no member of the Quincy clan except Dolly's Aunt Dorothy was able to get to Connecticut in time for the wedding. But with the colonies in a state of upheaval, even Dolly was willing to make concessions.

Once married, Dolly set about being a model wife. With good grace she accepted the fact that her honeymoon would consist only of the wearying, dusty journey from Fairfield to

Philadelphia. And once in Philadelphia, she conducted herself so diplomatically that even vinegar-tongued John Adams sang her praises to his own wife, Abigail: "Among a hundred men, almost, at this house, she lives and behaves with modesty, dignity, and discretion, I assure you. Her behavior is easy and genteel. She avoids talking about politics. In large and mixed companies she is totally silent, as a lady ought to be."

After a week's delay caused by the late arrival of many of the members, Congress finally reconvened. Georgia having at last sent delegates, all thirteen colonies were now represented for the first time. John Hancock was immediately swept up in a multitude of duties. On a typical day he would be in committee from seven to ten in the morning, then in Congress until four or five o'clock in the afternoon, and back in committee from six until ten in the evening.

In October Congress was thrown into confusion by the news that Dr. Benjamin Church had been unmasked as a traitor to the patriot cause. One of the earliest members of the Sons of Liberty, now Surgeon General of the Continental Army, Church had sold out to the British, spying on his friends and passing on their secrets to the enemy. When arrested, he was found to have in his possession a number of letters, one of them from a Loyalist in Boston.

"I have often told you what the dreams of your high-flaming sons would come to," the letter stated. "What says the Psalm-singer [Sam Adams] and Johnny Dupe [John Hancock] to fighting British troops now? They are at Philadelphia, I suppose, plotting more mischief. . . . You may depend upon it, government is determined to crush this rebellion. . . . You see Hancock and Adams are attainted already."

In Philadelphia, "the Psalm-singer" and "Johnny Dupe" were more stunned than any of their fellow Congressmen by the revelation of Church's treachery. For more than ten years Church had been their trusted comrade—lively, witty, and apparently dauntlessly courageous in the patriot cause. A few months earlier, when Hancock had asked Church to carry presents to Dolly in Fairfield, he had regarded the bland, smiling doctor as one of his closest friends. Now the man stood stripped, a blackguard who had sold out to the enemy.

Although Hancock and Sam Adams both received a full account of Church's trial and conviction, in their hearts they could scarcely admit the truth of the accusations. Indeed, in Congress, the two men spoke so leniently about Benjamin Church that they infuriated John Adams, who believed no punishment was too excessive for a traitor. After a brief imprisonment, Church was allowed to embark on a ship sailing to the West Indies. Fate exacted her own punishment: the ship vanished without a trace.

During the fall and winter the breach with England widened. Word arrived that King George III had rejected Congress's Olive Branch Petition and proclaimed the American colonies to be in open rebellion. The American general, Richard Montgomery, led an expedition against Canada and occupied Montreal. Then, by authorizing the formation of a navy, Congress took another step that alienated the colonies from the Crown.

The colonists had some stout defenders in England. The Whigs and Radicals in Parliament—Edmund Burke, Charles James Fox, and John Wilkes, among others—argued passionately in favor of conciliation. In the press, too, men spoke out for the Americans. "[The names] of Dickinson, Hancock, and Adams will vibrate through the earth," wrote a contributor to *The London Magazine*, "the defenders of their country, the assertors of the rights of mankind—and the immortal champions of liberty. . . . America will become the asylum of the world, and her victorious standard will fly with glory in the last."

As the breach with England widened, the split grew between Hancock and the two Adamses. Hancock still nursed a grievance over the way the two cousins had intrigued against him in proposing Washington as Commander-in-Chief of the Continental Army. The Adamses resented the friendship that had grown up between Hancock and the aristocrats from some of the other colonies, such men as John Dickinson of Pennsylvania, Robert R. Livingston of New York, and Benjamin Harrison of Virginia. These men, Sam Adams thought, were forming a faction hostile to the cause of independence. Actually, some of them were more hostile to the Adamses than they were to independence. Benjamin Harrison admitted as much in a letter to Washington, adding, however, that President Hancock was "quite of a different Cast, Noble, Disinterested and Generous to a very great Degree."

In November, the Hancocks were delighted to hear that Martha Washington was to spend a week in Philadelphia on the way to visit her husband in the camp at Cambridge. Dolly Hancock welcomed the prospect of a festive interlude; John and the other delegates had been working too hard to have much time for gaiety. A ball was scheduled in Mrs. Washington's honor at the City Tavern, but rumors began circulating that the Philadelphia Tories were preparing to create a disturbance if the ball were held. When the rumors reached the ears of businessman Christopher Marshall, he felt that action was necessary.

"I went to Col. Hancock's lodgings," Marshall related in his diary, "and finding he was not come from Congress, and the time grew short, being three o'clock, I walked up to the State House, in expectation of meeting him. That failing, I requested the door-keeper to call Samuel Adams, which he accordingly did, and he came.

"I then informed him of the account received of a ball, that was to be held this evening, and where, and that Mrs. Washington and Col. Hancock's wife were to be present. . . . I therefore requested he would give my respects to Col. Hancock, desire him to wait on Lady Washington to request her not to attend or go this evening. This he promised."

The ball was canceled, and as a result of the alarm, it was agreed that no balls would be held while troublesome times continued. The winter ahead seemed gloomier than ever to Dolly Quincy Hancock.

Just a few days before Christmas, Congress passed a resolution giving Washington permission to move against Boston, no matter what damage the town might suffer. In forwarding the proceedings to the Commander-in-Chief, Hancock wrote, "I would just inform you that the last resolve, relative to an attack upon Boston, passed after a most serious debate in a committee of the whole house. You are now left to the dictates of prudence and your own judgment." In closing, he noted. "May God crown your attempt with success. I most heartily wish it, though, individually, I may be the greatest sufferer."

In late January of the new year, 1776, General Henry Knox reached Cambridge, having achieved the seemingly impossible feat of hauling cannon and mortars overland through the snow from Fort Ticonderoga. These were the armaments Washington needed for an attack. Seizing Dorchester Heights, overlooking Boston, the Commander-in-Chief made ready to bombard the town. But before the actual shelling started, the British decided to evacuate, and by the middle of March all the redcoats had embarked on transports in Boston Harbor.

With the redcoats went more than a thousand Massachusetts Tories—tradesmen, mechanics, printers, sailors, and many of the colony's most brilliant men and aristocratic women. Thomas Hutchinson left, and Peter Oliver, and debonair Sam Quincy, Dolly Hancock's cousin and John's college friend. Dolly had lost someone even dearer to her some months before, when Attorney General Jonathan Sewall took passage for England with his wife, Esther, Dolly's sister. Also among the emigrants was John's cousin and former rival, William Bowes. Very few of those who sailed away ever returned to their native land.

As soon as the Continental Army took possession of the town, Washington hastened to send word to Philadelphia that the Hancock mansion had received no damage worth mentioning. A later message from Hancock's friend, Captain Cazneau, brought a more detailed report: the backgammon table from the library was missing, and the pasture fences had been burned for firewood, but everything else was in good order.

Hancock needed some cheerful news. For weeks he had been suffering from a continuing cold and fever, and one of his eyes was giving him great pain. Dolly was beginning to grow restless under the burden of clerical duties thrust upon her; she was more a secretary than a hostess. For months she had been kept busy packing up commissions to be sent off for the officers Congress had appointed, or using her dainty scissors to trim the rough edges off the bills of credit issued by Congress and signed by her husband.

One of Hancock's closest friends, Thomas Cushing, had been replaced as a delegate from Massachusetts by Elbridge Gerry. Cushing had been too outspoken in criticism of Sam Adams, and Adams had seen to it that he was kept at home as a member of the Massachusetts Council. Hancock still used him as a confidant. "I fear for the Defection of New York," John wrote; "the Spring will open before we are Ready, however, we must bestir ourselves. . . ."

Cushing also proved a useful agent for John Hancock. As chairman of the Marine Committee, Hancock was pushing the completion of two naval vessels being built in Massachusetts, the *Boston* and the *Hancock;* and he enlisted Cushing's help in the execution of their construction. He also asked Cushing's aid in obtaining a job for Eben Hancock, now unemployed. "I shall take it as a very particular favour if you would promote him," he wrote Cushing; "and with this I beg to Impress your mind, and pray use your Influence to have him Notic'd." Although Cushing could not oblige, a few weeks later John managed to wangle an appointment for Eben as deputy paymaster general for the eastern department of the Continental Army.

As time passed, Hancock was glad of Cushing's presence in Massachusetts, for his friend could keep him informed of the intrigues against him concocted by the Adams faction. The party in Massachusetts had split into the supporters of Hancock and the supporters of Sam Adams. Adams, with his Spartan ways, disapproved of Hancock's grand manner and strove to halt his ever-increasing popularity with the people at home by circulating rumors that the merchant prince of Beacon Hill was dissolute and profligate. Although deeply hurt, Hancock stoutly defended himself: "My utmost Exertions shall never be withheld for the Good of my Colony, whenever they can be usefull they shall be Employ'd in that Service however Dangerous, and I Defy Malice itself to Contradict the sincerity and uprightness of those Assertions."

Meanwhile, it had become increasingly evident that New York would probably be the next target for the British. Washington, after moving his troops down to Manhattan Island and Long Island, planned to journey on to Philadelphia to consult with Congress about the forthcoming campaign.

Hancock hastened to invite the Commander-in-Chief and Mrs. Washington to stay with him and Dolly during the visit. The Hancocks were now living at Arch and Fourth Streets, "an airy, open part of the city," very close to Christ Church and its cemetery. "As the house I live in is large and roomy," John wrote, "it will be entirely in Your power to live in that manner you should wish. Mrs. Washington may be as retired as she pleases. . . . I assure you, sir, I will do all in my power to render your stay agreeable and my house shall be entirely at your disposal."

Washington chose to lodge elsewhere, and Dolly was glad that he had not accepted the Hancocks' hospitality. She was expecting a child, and the prospect of a house full of guests did not give her much joy.

John, too, was relieved that his offer had not been taken up, for his heart was heavy with sadness. In April Aunt Lydia had died suddenly in Fairfield, while preparations were being made for her return to her home on Beacon Hill. The pressure of business in Congress had been so heavy that John, although "greatly Distress'd," was not able to get to Connecticut for the funeral. In these times of trial his life was at the service of his country, and personal grief would have to wait.

All throughout the spring of 1776 the movement toward independence gained strength. It was given great impetus by a short pamphlet, *Common Sense*, published in January and written by an Englishman, Thomas Paine, who had been in America only a few years. Hancock sent a copy to Cushing, noting that it "makes much Talk here." It made much talk because of its forceful call for immediate independence, and in less than three months it sold more than 100,000 copies. Its vivid, burning prose converted multitudes to its argument.

"Now is the seed-time of Continental union, faith and honour," Paine declared. "I challenge the warmest advocate for reconciliation to show a single advantage that this continent can reap by being connected with Great Britain. . . . England to Europe: America to itself."

On and on his resounding sentences went, attacking the British government and the King, arguing brilliantly and forcefully for independence. "I am not induced by motives of pride, party or resentment to espouse the doctrine of separation and independence; I am clearly, positively, and conscientiously persuaded that it is the true intent of this Continent to be so; that every thing short of *that* is mere patchwork, that it can afford no lasting felicity,—that it is leaving the sword to our children, and shrinking back at a time when a little more, a little further, would have rendered this Continent the glory of the earth."

Now, in the endless debates over which John Hancock presided with untiring tact, the clamor became more insistent for separation from Great Britain. Less and less heed was paid to the men who held that reconciliation should be attempted as soon as colonial grievances were settled. "The child Independence is now struggling for birth," Sam Adams said triumphantly. "I trust that in a short time it will be brought forth."

In April North Carolina specifically authorized its delegates to Congress to support "Independency." Less than a month later Congress passed a resolution urging that all colonies that had not yet set up their own governments should do so at once. Within the week Virginia sent word to its delegates that they should not only vote for independence, they should take the initiative in proposing that Congress make such a declaration.

On June 7, Richard Henry Lee of Virginia rose to his feet in the State House chamber to offer a resolution containing three main points:

> That these United Colonies are, and of right ought to be, free and independent States, that they are absolved from all allegiance to the British Crown, and that all political connection between them and the State of Great Britain is, and ought to be, totally dissolved.

> That it is expedient forthwith to take the most effectual measures for forming foreign Alliances.

> That a plan of confederation be prepared and transmitted to the respective Colonies for their consideration and approbation.

In the debate that followed, John Adams was one of those to take the lead in proposing that the resolution be adopted, but there was strong opposition from the delegates representing Pennsylvania, New York, and South Carolina.

John Hancock had now reached his own decision. Events had carried the country—and him—too far now to turn back. Negotiations for a reconciliation had failed; King George III had shown little desire to remedy the wrongs that had been done. Hancock thought back to a recent letter from his father-in-law, Edmund Quincy, quoting the great English lawyer, Blackstone: "When protection ceaseth, allegiance ceaseth to be the duty of subjects."

For more than a decade Hancock had insisted upon his rights as an Englishman. Since these rights were not to be allowed to him and his countrymen by the Crown, Hancock was resolved to seek them as an American. He would have preferred reconciliation, but reconciliation was obviously out of the question, and as President of Congress he should set an example to the faint of heart. Whatever his differences with the two Adams cousins, he now stood with them on the issue of independence.

On Monday, June 10, no agreement could be reached in the debate. At last the opposing factions agreed to postpone a formal vote for three weeks, to Monday, July 1. In the meantime, it was resolved that a committee should be appointed to draft a Declaration of Independence, in case the vote should be in the affirmative. The rawboned, redheaded Thomas Jefferson of Virginia, John Adams of Massachusetts, Benjamin Franklin of Pennsylvania, Roger Sherman of Connecticut, and Robert Livingston of New York were named to the committee. A second committee was appointed to "prepare a plan of treaties to be proposed to foreign powers," and a third committee was elected to draw up a plan of confederation for the colonies.

The next day Hancock hastened to send word of these dramatic happenings to Washington. "We have been two days in a Committee of the whole," he wrote, "deliberating on three capital matters, the most important in their nature of any that have yet been before us, and have sat till seven oclock in the evening each day."

While the three committees set about their history-making tasks, John Hancock, as President of Congress, was inundated by the thousand-and-one routine details involved in keeping the machinery of government moving. An attack by the British on New York was believed imminent; instructions had to be sent to Washington and to the New Jersey government. The naval vessels being built in Massachusetts required constant correspondence. Messages brought by postriders had to be opened, read, and answered. Commissions had to be signed, bills of credit issued. (By now Hancock had enlisted the aid of a clerk, so Dolly no longer devoted hours to trimming the rough edges off the bills with her scissors.)

In the midst of all this drudgery, a letter from Cushing brought news that the Massachusetts legislature had appointed Hancock a major general. It also contained an unhappy revelation: in the May elections, Hancock had been left out of both the Massachusetts House and the Council, although he remained a delegate to Congress. Obviously Sam and John Adams and their supporters had been successful in whittling away at his popularity. "I think I do not merit such Treatment," he protested, "but my Exertions and my Life are and shall be at their Service."

On July 1, a hot, cloudless day, the delegates assembled in the cool white-paneled chamber in the State House to continue the debate about independence. This day, as on frequent other occasions, the Congress resolved itself into a "committee of the whole." This meant that President Hancock would leave the Chair, surrendering it to a newly appointed Chairman of the Committee. The debate and vote that followed would be unofficial, and at the conclusion the President would resume the Chair for the final vote.

After several matters of routine business had been attended to, John Hancock with great ceremony handed the mace to the clerk and took his place in a seat on the floor of the chamber. His friend, portly Benjamin Harrison of Virginia, assumed the role of Chairman of the Committee, and the debate began. Slowly, carefully, John Dickinson began to speak. No one could deny his sincerity. The colonies were not yet ready for independence, he felt. They were unprepared, poor and poorly armed, unable to support themselves or defend themselves. Then John Adams rose. His speech was concise, logical, persuasive, powerful. His argument for independence swept all John Dickinson's eloquence before it.

When Adams finished speaking, the vote was taken. Nine of the thirteen colonies were in the affirmative. New York abstained, Delaware was split, and Pennsylvania and South Carolina voted against the resolution. As Congress was still sitting as a committee of the whole, it was decided to defer the final vote until the next day.

There was feverish activity that warm summer night as the Massachusetts delegates took the lead in trying to bring round the reluctant members from Pennsylvania and South Carolina. At last the men from South Carolina agreed to vote in the affirmative, and the two Pennsylvania delegates most heartily opposed to independence, John Dickinson and Robert Morris, agreed not to take their seats on the following day.

On July 2, with periodic squalls of rain beating against the windows of the State House chamber, President Hancock again turned over the Chair to Benjamin Harrison, and another vote was taken. Dickinson and Morris kept their word, and the Pennsylvania delegation was counted in favor of the resolution. South Carolina voted in favor. Then the doors of the chamber burst open, and Caesar Rodney of Delaware burst in, spattered with rain and mud, having ridden eighty miles on horseback to arrive in time to bring his colony into the camp of independence. New York, awaiting word from a convention at home, still abstained. John Hancock resumed the Chair as President. The committee of the whole recommended to Congress that a formal vote be taken. It was unanimous for the twelve colonies that voted, and within two weeks New York, too, spoke in the affirmative.

As soon as the vote on independence had been taken, Congress again resolved itself into a committee of the whole to consider the written Declaration of Independence drafted by Thomas Jefferson. For the rest of Tuesday, all day Wednesday, and on into Thursday, July 4, the delegates considered Jefferson's draft, sentence by sentence, paragraph by paragraph, page by page. A word was taken out here, added there. A passage blaming the slave trade solely on King George III was struck out. Several phrases considered too hostile to the British people as a whole were deleted. But what was finally adopted by the whole Congress on July 4 was substantially the Declaration of Independence as Thomas Jefferson had written it.

After the document had been ratified, John Hancock, as President of Congress, took quill pen in hand and signed it with his customary flourish. His signature was attested to by Secretary Charles Thomson. By next morning the Declaration of Independence had been printed, and soon it was being carried by couriers to all parts of the new United States of America.

For nearly thirty days John Hancock's signature stood alone with Thomson's on the document. Not until August 2, when the engrossed copy on parchment had been prepared, did the other delegates affix their signatures, and some of them actually did not sign until much later than that.

Hancock had now made his final choice as a patriot, placing himself beyond any possible leniency on the part of King George III if the rebellion failed. While Charles Thomson might have escaped harsh punishment on the grounds that he was acting merely as an official clerk, John Hancock could not hope that any such excuse would be accepted from him. Long since, he had been singled out as an arch-rebel, and now his name, written large and bold, stood at the bottom of a document which, in the eyes of the British government, was an open declaration of treason.

Two days later, when sending a copy of the Declaration to George Washington, Hancock wrote, "Altho it is not possible to foresee the Consequences of Human Actions, yet it is nevertheless a Duty we owe ourselves and Posterity, in all our public Counsels, to decide in the best Manner we are able, and to leave the Event to that Being who controuls both Causes and Events to bring about his own Determination. Impressed with this Sentiment, and at the same Time fully convinced, that our Affairs may take a more favourable Turn, the Congress have judged it necessary to dissolve the Connection between Great Britain and the American Colonies, and to declare them free & independent States. . . ."

This letter and others written by Hancock at this time show little of the exhilaration over the Declaration that the correspondence of John Adams and Sam Adams so vividly displays. Sam Adams had been driven by a burning passion for independence; John Adams was moved no less intensely by a cool logic; both men were shapers of events. John Hancock, on the other hand, had allowed himself to be shaped by events, to be led by his heart rather than his head. Yet, when Hancock saw his duty, no man could have been more unflagging in dedication, more unswerving in courage. If, as his enemies charged, he tried too hard to be well liked, it was a trait that would find its counterpart in the American character for generations to come. In signing the Declaration of Independence he had taken a bold stand, but he knew that the ties to England—commerce, language, religion, laws, affections—could not be severed without pain as well as joy.

On July 8 the Declaration of Independence was proclaimed in Philadelphia. It was a "warm sunshine morning," according to businessman Christopher Marshall, who, with the members of Philadelphia's Committee of Inspection and Committee of Safety, "went in a body to the State House Yard, where, in the presence of a great concourse of people, the Declaration of Independence was read by John Nixon. The company declared their approbation by three repeated huzzas. The King's Arms were taken down in the Court Room, State House at the same time. . . . Fine starlight, pleasant evening. There were bonfires, ringing bells, with other great demonstrations of joy upon the unanimity and agreement of the declaration."

Within the next few weeks the Declaration of Independence would be proclaimed throughout the thirteen new states to scenes of similar joy and jubilation. Meanwhile, having set this historic machinery in operation, Presdent Hancock and the members of the Continental Congress settled down to the business of running a new country.

About this time an outbreak of smallpox aroused fear of an epidemic, and citizens and soldiers alike were rushing to be inoculated. When Hancock learned that John Adams was worried over how his family back in Braintree would fare during inoculation, Hancock, disregarding Adams's recent antagonism, generously offered Abigail Adams and her children the use of the Beacon Hill mansion and its staff as a hospital. John Adams, with characteristic practicality, accepted the offer.

Hancock's home in Philadelphia also had its quota of patients, among them Katy Quincy, Dolly's sister. Katy, John wrote Cushing, "has been Inoculated, and has it exceeding full, but is upon the Recovery, she will have enough to Convince her Friends she will not Take it again."

August 2, the day when the engrossed copy of the Declaration was ready, turned out to be a sweltering day. Even the chamber in the State House where the delegates assembled seemed like an oven. The men who gathered were not, in all cases, the men who had voted for independence a month earlier. Some delegates had gone home; new ones had arrived to take their place. But John Hancock still served as President of Congress.

Now that the New York delegation had received instructions to cast their vote for independence, the document was called "The unanimous Declaration of the thirteen united States of America." When the parchment was presented, Hancock did not hesitate. In a bold hand he wrote out his signature in the same large copperplate script he used on his personal letters—perhaps a slight bit larger, in keeping with the great importance of the event. For the second time, he put his name to a document that could cost him his life. Although the records of the Continental Congress give no hint of what was said on this momentous occasion, tradition has it that Hancock, throwing down the pen, remarked, "There! John Bull can read my name without spectacles, and may now double his reward of £500 for my head. *That* is my defiance."

Then he is supposed to have turned to the other delegates and said, "We must be unanimous. There must be no pulling different ways; we must all hang together."

To this Benjamin Franklin allegedly answered, "Yes, we must, indeed, all hang together, or most assuredly we shall all hang separately."

Hanging loomed large in the minds of the delegates. Although Independence had been declared, it still had to be won, and the prospect seemed increasingly dubious. On July 3 General William Howe landed more than 9,000 redcoats on Staten

Island, and on the twelfth Admiral Lord Richard Howe arrived with a strong fleet. By the end of August the Howes succeeded in driving the Continental Army off Long Island, and in mid-September the redcoats triumphantly took possession of New York.

Realizing that the new nation's first hours could scarcely seem darker, John Hancock, as President of Congress, sent an eloquent plea to the thirteen United States. "Let us convince our enemies," he wrote, "that, as we are entered into the present contest for the defense of our liberties, so we are resolved, with the firmest reliance on Heaven for the justice of our cause, never to relinquish it, but rather to perish in the ruins of it.

"If we do but remain firm—if we are not dismayed at the little shocks of fortune, and are determined, at all hazards, that we will be free,—I am persuaded under the gracious smiles of Providence, assisted by our own most strenuous endeavors, we shall finally succeed, agreeably to our wishes, and thereby establish the independence, the happiness, and the glory of the United States of America."

With these ringing sentences John Hancock spoke for himself as well as for Congress. A decade earlier, as an Englishman, he had plunged into a struggle to defend his rights and the rights of his fellow colonists. There had been shocks of fortune: he had watched his great mercantile enterprises come to a standstill and seen his home, his stores, his wharf occupied by the soldiers of his King. He had braved all hazards and placed his life in jeopardy. Now he no longer struggled as an Englishman; he fought as an American. In these times of perilous trial, "the independence, the happiness, and the glory of the United States of America" seemed a long way off, but, like his fellow Americans, he was determined to perish rather than relinquish the dream of freedom.

XV

The Closing Years

"I am almost worn out," Hancock confessed to his friend Cushing not long after the signing of the Declaration of Independence. "My Duty is Constant, I have hardly time for necessary Rest."

As 1776 rolled to a close, President Hancock was faced with mounting tribulations. The delegates to Congress squabbled with each other. Congress, in turn, squabbled with the governments of the new states. And the redcoats inflicted defeat after defeat on the shabby, hungry troops of the Continental Army. Fearing an attack on Philadelphia. Congress fled to Baltimore, then returned to the City of Brotherly Love early in 1777, after Washington's coups at Trenton and Princeton temporarily stemmed the British advance.

Although John Hancock had just passed his fortieth birthday, he now seemed old beyond his years. Gout and a nervous affliction gave him increasing trouble. He was still a man to cause female hearts to flutter, but his shoulders had more of a stoop than ever, and his face looked drawn and haggard.

He had one reason for great joy. A short time before the

153

flight to Baltimore, Dolly had given birth to a daughter, whom her proud parents named in honor of Aunt Lydia. "I have sent everywhere to get a gold or silver rattle for the child with a coral to send, but cannot get one," wrote John to Dolly, who had delayed returning to Philadelphia from Baltimore. "I will have one if possible on yr. coming. I have sent a sash for her & two little papers of pins for you. . . . I shall make out as well as I can, but I assure you, my Dear Soul, I long to have you here. . . . When I part from you again it must be a very extraordinary occasion."

When Dolly at last was prepared to travel, John dashed about making preparations for her transportation along the muddy roads. "I wish I could do better for you," he told her, "but we must Ruff it." His duties continued to make his life hectic. "I am so harassed with applications, & have been sending off Expresses to Call all the Members here, that I have as much as I can Turn my hands to; I don't get down to dinner, Catch a Bit, I write, & then at it again . . . if it promotes the cause I am happy.

"Jo comes in with a plate of minc'd Veal, that I must stop, I shall take the plate in one hand, the knife in the other, without cloath, or any Comfort, & Eat a little & then to writing, for I have not Room on the Table to put a plate, I am up to the eyes in papers."

Rumors, he said, were rife that the British Army was about to leave New York. "One thing I know that they can't at present come here. . . . Never fear, we shall get the day finally with the smiles of heaven. Do Take precious Care of our dear little Lydia."

It was a blissful day for the Hancocks when they were at last reunited, but their happiness soon changed to the deepest sorrow. In August, despite the precious care that was lavished upon her, little Lydia died.

For weeks to follow, all trace of splendor and vitality vanished from John Hancock's manner. His face ravaged by grief, he went about his tasks like a man in a stupor. And he had no chance for rest. By the end of September General William Howe's redcoats had occupied Philadelphia, forcing Congress to flee to Lancaster and then on to the little town of York. The starving, ragged Continental Army made plans to take up winter quarters on a bleak plateau twenty-odd miles northwest of Philadelphia, at a spot called Valley Forge.

Knowing that the two armies soon would be immobilized by snow and icy weather, that the war would drag itself to a standstill, Hancock decided to take two or three months' leave of absence from his duties. At the end of October, 1777, he bid a temporary farewell to the Congress he had selflessly served for two-and-a-half years.

"As I could never flatter myself your choice proceeded from any idea of my abilities," he said in his closing address, "but rather from a partial opinion of my attachment to the liberties of America, I felt myself under the strongest obligations to discharge the duties of the office, and I accepted the appointment with the firmest resolutions to go through the business annexed to it in the best manner I was able. Every argument conspired to make me exert myself, and I endeavored by industry and attention to make up for every other deficiency. . . . I pray Heaven that unanimity & perseverance may go hand in hand in this house, and that everything which may tend to distract or divide your councils be forever banished."

Despite his heartfelt wish for unanimity, Congress was immediately divided over the question of whether or not to give Hancock a vote of thanks for his service. Sam Adams tried to block the proposal. At heart even more of a Puritan than his cousin John Adams, he believed that no man should be singled out for special homage, especially a man such as Hancock, with his grand manner and extravagant ways. There were some, however, who said that what Sam Adams mistrusted most about Hancock was his popularity among the people of Massachusetts. In any event, his exertions were in vain. The vote of thanks was passed, and the long-standing enmity between the two former friends grew more bitter.

The months in Congress had brought both Hancock and Adams to crucial points in their careers. Sam Adams had begun to fade in importance and influence. As a delegate he had frequently been charged with creating dissension, quarrels, and antagonism, with lacking the qualities of statesmanship that distinguished his cousin John Adams or the young Virginian, Thomas Jefferson. He seemed to know a great deal about overthrowing an old government, but not much about building a new one.

As President of Congress, John Hancock had proved himself an industrious worker and an admirable diplomatist, but he had not displayed the intellectual brilliance that a young nation needed. Back in Massachusetts, however, he was regarded as a hero almost without peer. The propaganda machine by which Sam Adams had toppled Thomas Hutchinson seemed increasingly ineffectual when turned against the powerful politician of Beacon Hill.

Escorted by a party of light dragoons, Hancock set out from Philadelphia on the long journey home to Boston, his foot wrapped in baize to ease his suffering from gout. During the third week in November, he and Dolly reached Boston, to be welcomed by the ringing of bells and the firing of cannon. Less than two weeks later Sam Adams' arrival in town went almost unnoticed.

Despite his ill health, Hancock plunged into a whirl of activity. The great stone mansion was renovated, and a large wooden wing was built for banquets and entertainments. He took an important part in the town meetings, and in January, 1778, he presided over the Massachusetts convention which approved the Articles of Confederation, the plan of union for the new national government.

Because Dolly was expecting their second child, John kept postponing his return to Congress. The baby, born in May, was christened John George Washington Hancock, and the proud father soon set off for York, Pennsylvania, where Congress was meeting. Although he served this time as an ordinary delegate, Hancock was no less scrupulous in his devotion to his duties. And, after the day's work was done, he penned letter after letter to the wife he adored. "I embrace the oppor'y of writing you, altho' I wrote you Two Letters the Day before yesterday, & this is my Seventh Letter, & not one word have I heard from you. . . . I hope this will meet you tolerably Recover'd from your late Confinement, I wish to hear of your being below Stairs & able to take the care of our Dear little one. I am much concern'd about your improving the fine Season in Riding. . . . as soon as we have got over the important Business now before Congress I shall solicit leave to Return home."

Within a short time he was back in Boston, his career as a member of Congress now virtually at an end. In May, 1779, he returned as a delegate for a few weeks only. In 1785, although elected President of Congress, he was too crippled by gout to travel, and he resigned without assuming his seat.

Meanwhile, soon after arriving back in Boston in August, 1778, Hancock was at last able to indulge his desire to lead troops into combat. As a major general in the Massachusetts militia, he took part in an abortive Franco-American attack on the British forces at Newport, Rhode Island. Even though his political enemies tried to imply that he behaved more like a boy with toy soldiers than a competent military leader, his popularity with the people of Massachusetts remained undiminished.

And when the citizens of the Commonwealth of Massachusetts elected their first Governor in 1780, John Hancock was their choice. His generosity and charity were only two reasons for his continuing popularity. To the people he symbolized the aristocrat who was a democrat at heart; for the times in which he lived it was an appealing combination. Having cast off the King and the Royal Governor, the common man found that John Hancock supplied a goodly amount of the pomp, pageantry, and authority they had been raised to expect. And his devotion to the principles of liberty was something not even his most hostile foes could effectively disparage.

Sam Adams took a dubious view of the people's choice. "I . . . wish with all my heart," he confided to Mrs. Adams, "he may distinguish between his real friends and his flattering enemies; or, rather, between the real friends of the country and those who will be ready to offer the essence of flattery to him who is the first man in it."

All Adams's misgivings were confirmed by the series of parties and balls with which Hancock celebrated his inauguration. "I am afraid there is more pomp and parade than is consistent with the sober republican principle with which the framers of it thought they had founded it," Adams declared. "Why should this new era be introduced with entertainments expensive, and tending to dissipate the minds of the people? Does it become us to lead the people to such public diversions as promote superfluity of dress and ornament, when it is as much as they can bear to support the expense of clothing a naked army?"

Despite the attacks of Adams and his followers, Hancock's position was impregnable. At each of the annual elections he was returned to office by an overwhelming majority.

When the war finally drew to a close, John dispatched a heartfelt letter to his old friend Captain James Scott. "I have for ten years past devoted myself to the concern of the Public," he wrote. "I have not the vanity to think that I have been of very extensive service in our late unhappy contest, but one thing I can truly Boast, I sat out upon honest Principles & strictly adhered to them to the close of the contest, and this I defy malice itself to controvert. I have lost many thousand sterlg, but, thank God, my country is saved and by the smile of Heaven I am a free & Independent man."

Informing Scott that he is rebuilding a store that the British had burned to ashes, he announced his intention of resuming business activities the following spring. "I am determined," he declared, "in the course of this month to resign my command of this Commonwealth & return to private life, after the many fatigues I have gone thro'. . . . I am really worn out with public business."

But public life held a fascination he could not resist, and even though his letter to Scott was written in 1783, he did not resign until 1785. By that time his attacks of gout were becoming excruciatingly painful, and his nerves seemed constantly on edge. For days on end he was forced to keep to his bed in a darkened room. One attack was so painful that he had to be carried from his carriage to the sofa in the drawing room, where servants cut his clothing off to relieve the pressure on his horribly swollen limbs.

Just about the time he resigned as Governor, Hancock made a gesture toward settling a long-standing squabble with Harvard College. Certain funds had been entrusted to him a dozen years earlier when he was appointed college treasurer. The securities themselves he had returned late in 1776, and his gesture in 1785 was to submit a long overdue accounting, which indicated that he owed Harvard a trifle more than £1,000. For part of this period he had neglected his own affairs as well as those of Harvard, but his main reason for the delay in giving an accounting seems simply to have been a stubborn resistance to being hounded about the matter.

Politically, Hancock had made an astute move by resigning

in 1785. The following year his successor, James Bowdoin, was faced with an uprising by farmers and small property holders, burdened by taxes and duties imposed in an attempt to pay off Massachusetts' share of the national debt. To forestall further foreclosure of their homes and farms, the debtors rallied around Daniel Shays and marched against the courts, determined to close them up. Not until early in 1787 was the rebellion quelled.

A few weeks after the end of Shays' Rebellion, John Hancock announced that he was again a candidate for the governorship. At the election he rolled back into office with more than 75 per cent of the vote.

The burdens of public office provided a welcome distraction from his personal anguish. In January a tragic blow had fallen upon him and Dolly. With his son, John George Washington Hancock, he and a friend had been strolling along the main street of a Massachusetts village. In a store window the eight-year-old boy had seen a pair of ice skates. The friend bought them for him, over the father's protests. Young John put the skates on immediately, tried them out on the icy pavement, and fell, striking his head. The fall proved fatal. John confessed himself almost "totally deranged" over the boy's death; his grief was deepened by the knowledge that, at fifty, he probably would not produce another heir.

Hancock returned to public life in time to render another significant service to his country. Late in 1787 Congress sent the newly formulated Constitution to the state legislatures for submission to special ratifying conventions. The approval of nine states was needed before the document could go into effect. Because of its strength and size, Massachusetts was regarded as a key state; yet the Anti-Federalists, as opponents of the Constitution were known, were stronger in the state than the Federalists, who advocated adoption of the Constitution. It was widely rumored that neither John Hancock nor Samuel

Adams was enthusiastic about the new document. Both men, despite their individual differences, seemed united in their belief that strong state governments were preferable to a strong central government.

Elected chairman of the ratifying convention in January, 1788, Hancock was absent from most of the sessions because of illness. In the meantime, the Federalists managed to convince him that ratification of the Constitution was essential to the preservation of the country, and they further placated him by promising to support amendments guaranteeing popular liberties. Finally the ailing Governor, wrapped in flannels, was carried into the convention by friends. Rising with difficulty to his feet, he delivered an eloquent oration urging that the Constitution be ratified with certain amendments, most of which were later incorporated into the Bill of Rights. His persuasive speech swung the convention; Massachusetts ratified the Constitution by a vote of 187 to 168, a narrow margin, but a decisive one.

Having given his support to a national government, Hancock now set out to campaign for the Vice-Presidency. Washington, he knew, would undoubtedly garner the most electoral votes and secure the Presidency. But the candidate with the second largest number of electoral votes would become Vice President, and Governor Hancock had high hopes that that man would be himself. Throughout 1788 he campaigned vigorously, but during the fall he was frequently immobilized by gout, and outside of Massachusetts he began to lose ground. When the ballots were counted in April, 1789, Hancock ran fifth among eleven candidates; the first Vice President of the United States of America was to be John Adams.

Hancock was disappointed but not embittered by the defeat. He remained the most powerful man in the most powerful state in the Union, and in the annual Massachusetts elections of 1789 he was returned to the governorship by a thundering majority. And, with Hancock's backing, Sam Adams was elected Lieutenant Governor. A common hostility toward the Federalists had helped the two men bury their enmity toward each other. Moreover, Adams had come to realize he must have Hancock's support if he were to hope for any important political office in Massachusetts. With characteristic generosity, the Governor forgave the many injuries Adams had done him. At the inauguration the two men appeared in identical suits of American broadcloth, a gesture to advertise and encourage domestic manufacturing.

In the fall of 1789 Governor Hancock found himself at odds with President Washington. During a tour of New England Washington visited Boston, and the two clashed over a question of protocol: should the Governor of Massachusetts call upon the President of the United States, or should the President of the United States call upon the Governor of Massachusetts?

When Washington entered the town, Hancock, pleading illness, failed to greet him in person. The Governor undoubtedly was ill, but there were additional reasons for his not appearing. Even though he had thrown his weight behind ratification of the Constitution, he remained an ardent supporter of states' rights, especially the right of a Governor to take precedence over the President. Moreover, when President of Congress, Hancock had become accustomed to giving orders to Washington, then Commander-in-Chief of the Continental Army.

Washington made no secret of his irritation over Hancock's lack of deference. Almost at once he dispatched a messenger stating that he would be unable to dine at the Beacon Hill mansion, as previously planned. There matters rested overnight, and the next day states' rights gave way to the national government. Shortly after noon, swathed in bandages, Hancock had himself carried on a litter to Washington's quarters.

The question of precedence had been settled: no other state governor ventured a similar test.

To the people of Massachusetts, however, Hancock remained supreme. At each annual election he continued to win the governorship, and he carried along Sam Adams as Lieutenant Governor. The old comrades now were as close as they had been in the dramatic days leading up to the Revolution.

By the time John Hancock reached his fifty-sixth birthday, however, it was evident that his days were numbered. Much of the time he was confined to bed or to a wheelchair, his feet and hands so swollen with gout that he was in an agony of pain. And when he was able to appear in public, he tottered about like an infirm old man. On the morning of October 8, 1793, he suddenly experienced difficulty in breathing, and within an hour he was dead.

For nearly a week the body of Governor Hancock lay in state in the great stone mansion on Beacon Hill, and thousands of mourners filed through the imposing doorway to pay tribute to one of the nation's greatest patriots. Here lay the man who had been the merchant prince of Boston, who had thrown his fortune behind the fight for liberty and hazarded his life, the man who had served as President of the Provincial Congress and, with Samuel Adams, been excluded from General Gage's proffer of amnesty. Here lay the man who, for two-and-a-half grueling years, had served selflessly as President of the Continental Congress, guiding the discordant delegates at a time of crisis. Torn between his loyalties as an Englishman and his conviction that the rights and privileges of his fellow countrymen must be secured, he had finally taken the path toward separation from Great Britain. He had become the first Governor of the Commonwealth of Massachusets, re-elected many times. His influence had helped obtain ratification of the Constitution in a pivotal state. Here, in the most splendid home in Boston, now draped in black and crowded with grieving throngs, lay the man who, each time the moment for decision arrived, had unfailingly made a patriot's choice.

The funeral was the most impressive that New England had ever witnessed. More than 20,000 people marched in the procession, which moved from the Beacon Hill mansion across the Common and down Frog Lane to the Liberty Pole, standing on the spot of the Liberty Tree, which the redcoats had chopped down. Then the mourners moved through Main Street and around the Old State House, once the Town House, and then on to the Old Granary Burying Ground.

Ahead of the pallbearers marched the new Governor, seventy-one-year-old Sam Adams, shaken by palsy and forced by fatigue to turn back before the cemetery was reached. The Vice President of the United States, John Adams, marched farther back. Behind the bier rode Dolly Hancock, who, within three years, would marry Hancock's faithful friend, Captain James Scott; remarkably pretty and vivacious, Dolly would live to be eighty-two.

For more than a century John Hancock's grave was marked only by a rough stone reading, "No. 16 Tomb of Hancock." But the patriot needed no marble monument to recall his deeds to future generations. His name endured, written large and bold, the first signature beneath the final words of the Declaration of Independence: "We mutually pledge to each other our Lives, our Fortunes and our sacred Honour." It was a pledge John Hancock upheld to the very end.

Bibliography

NOTE: Books suggested for further reading are denoted by *. A list of *Additional Suggestions for Further Reading* may be found following these sources.

I. PRIMARY MATERIAL ON JOHN HANCOCK

Adams, John. *Diary and Autobiography of John Adams.* (Vols. 1-4 in Series I of The Adams Papers, L. H. Butterfield, Editor-in-Chief.) Cambridge, Mass.: Harvard University Press, 1961.

——. *The Works of John Adams, Second President of the United States.* Edited by Charles Francis Adams. 10 vols. Boston: Little, Brown and Company, 1856.

Adams, John and Abigail. *Familiar Letters of John Adams and His Wife Abigail Adams During the Revolution.* Edited by Charles Francis Adams. New York: Hurd and Houghton, 1876.

Adams, John and Abigail *et al. Adams Family Correspondence.* (Vols. 1-2 in Series II of The Adams Papers, L. H. Butterfield, Editor-in-Chief.) Cambridge, Mass.: Harvard University Press, 1963.

Adams, Samuel. *The Writings of Samuel Adams.* Collected and Edited by Harry Alonzo Cushing. 4 vols. New York and London: G. P. Putnam's Sons, 1904-1908.

American Antiquarian Society. *Proceedings.* New Series: Vols. XII (1899), XV (1904), XXXV (1926), L (1941). Worcester, Mass.: Published by the Society.

Barker, John. *The British in Boston: Being the Diary of Lieutenant John Barker of the King's Own Regiment from November 15, 1774 to May 31, 1776.* Edited by Elizabeth Ellery Dana. Cambridge, Mass.: Harvard University Press, 1924.

Bates, Samuel A., Editor. *Records of the Town of Braintree, 1640-1793.* Randolph, Mass.: Daniel H. Huxford, 1886.

Brown, Abram English. *John Hancock: His Book.* Boston: Lee and Shepard, 1898.

Burnett, Edmund C., Editor. *Letters of Members of the Continental Congress.* 8 vols. Washington, D.C.: Carnegie Institution of Washington, 1921-1936.

Colonial Society of Massachusetts, The. *Publications.* Vols. VI (1904), XXXIV (1943). Boston: Published by the Society.

Connecticut Historical Society. *Collections.* Vol. II (1870). Hartford: Published for the Society.

Curwen, Samuel. *Journal and Letters of the Late Samuel Curwen.* Second Edition. Edited by George Atkinson Ward. London: Wiley and Putnam, 1844.

Force, Peter, Editor. *American Archives.* Fourth Series: Vols. II (1839), IV (1843), V (1844), VI (1846). Fifth Series: I (1848). Washington, D.C.: M. St. Clair Clarke and Peter Force.

Ford, Worthington Chauncey, Editor. *Journals of the Continental Congress.* 34 vols. Washington, D.C.: Government Printing Office, 1904-1937.

Franklin, Benjamin. *The Works of Benjamin Franklin.* Edited by Jared Sparks. 10 vols. Boston: Whittemore, Niles, and Hall, 1856.

Hancock, John. Manuscripts. Mellen Chamberlain Collection. Boston Public Library.

*———. "Oration, Delivered at Boston, March 5, 1774." *The Magazine of History,* Vol. 24 (1923), No. 1.

———. "A John Hancock Letter Written When Congress Was Leaving Baltimore Town." *Maryland Historical Magazine,* December, 1952.

———. "A John Hancock Letter to Thomas Cushing." *Old-Time New England,* October, 1923.

Harlequin. "On the Civil War in America." *The London Magazine,* August, 1775.

Heath, William. *Memoirs of Major-General Heath.* Boston: I. Thomas and E. T. Andrews, 1798.

Hutchinson, Thomas. *The Diary and Letters of His Excellency Thomas Hutchinson, Esq.* Edited by Peter Orlando Hutchinson. 2 vols. Boston: Houghton, Mifflin & Co., 1884-1886.

———. *The History of the Province of Massachusetts Bay.* Vol. III. London: John Murray, 1828.

Marshall, Christopher. *Passages from the Remembrancer of Christopher Marshall.* Edited by William Duane, Jr. Philadelphia: Printed by James Crissy, 1839.

Massachusetts Historical Society. *Collections.* First Series: Vol. V (1798). Fifth Series: Vols. III (1877), IV (1878). Sixth Series: Vol. IV (1801). Seventh Series: Vols. IV (1904), LXXI (1914). Boston: Published by the Society.

———. *Proceedings.* First Series: Vols. III (1859), V (1862), VIII (1866). Second Series: Vols. I (1885), VI (1891), XVI (1903). Third Series: Vols. XLIII (1910), XLVIII (1915), LV (1923), LX (1927), LXII (1930), LXIII (1931). Boston: Published by the Society.

"Memoirs of John Hancock, Esq." *The New Lottery Magazine; or, Fortunate Repository,* August, 1776.

Myers, Theodorus Bailey, Editor. *Letters and Manuscripts of All the*

Signers of the Declaration of Independence. New York: Privately printed, 1871.

The New England Historical and Genealogical Register. Vols. XI (1857), XII (1858), XIX (1865), XXII (1868), LXXXIV (1930). Boston: Published by Samuel G. Drake and others.

New-York Historical Society. *Collections.* Publication Fund Series: Vol. XI (1879). New York: Published for the Society.

Phinney, Elias. *History of the Battle at Lexington.* Boston: Phelps and Farnham, 1825.

Pynchon, William. *The Diary of William Pynchon of Salem.* Edited by Fitch Edward Oliver. Boston and New York: Houghton, Mifflin and Company, 1890.

Rodney, Caesar. *Letters to and from Caesar Rodney.* Edited by George Herbert Ryden. Philadelphia: The University of Pennsylvania Press, 1933.

Rowe, John. *Letters and Diary of John Rowe, Boston Merchant.* Edited by Anne Rowe Cunningham. Boston: W. B. Clarke Company, 1903.

Salisbury, Edward E. *Family Memorials.* New Haven: Privately printed, 1885.

Scott, James. "Letter to John Hancock." *Old-Time New England,* July, 1934.

Sparks, Jared, Editor. *Correspondence of the American Revolution.* 4 vols. Boston: Little, Brown, and Company, 1853.

Sumner, William H. "Reminiscences." *The New England Historical and Genealogical Register,* Vol. VIII (1854).

Thatcher, Benjamin B. *Traits of the Tea Party; Being a Memoir of George R. T. Hewes.* New York: Harper & Brothers, 1835.

Washington, George. *The Writings of George Washington.* Edited by John C. Fitzpatrick. 39 vols. Washington, D.C.: Government Printing Office, 1931-1944.

Watkins, Walter K. "How the British Left the Hancock House." *Old-Time New England,* April, 1923.

Watson, Elkanah. *Men and Times of the Revolution.* Second Edition. Edited by Winslow C. Watson. New York: Dana and Company, 1857.

II. SECONDARY MATERIAL ON JOHN HANCOCK

Abbott, Katharine M. *Old Paths and Legends of New England.* New York and London: G. P. Putnam's Sons, 1903.

Adams, James Truslow. "Portrait of an Empty Barrel." *Harper's Magazine,* September, 1930.

Allan, Herbert S. *John Hancock: Patriot in Purple.* New York: The Macmillan Company, 1948.

Baxter, W. T. *The House of Hancock: Business in Boston, 1724-1775.* Cambridge, Mass.: Harvard University Press, 1945.

* Bowen, Catherine Drinker. *John Adams and the American Revolution*. Boston: Little, Brown and Company, 1950.

Bridenbaugh, Carl. *Cities in Revolt: Urban Life in America, 1743-1776*. New York: Alfred A. Knopf, 1955.

Burnett, Edmund Cody. *The Continental Congress*. New York: The Macmillan Company, 1941.

Burrage, William Clarence. *John Hancock and His Times*. Boston: John Hancock Mutual Life Insurance Co., 1891.

Cary, John. *Joseph Warren: Physician, Politician, Patriot*. Urbana: University of Illinois Press, 1961.

* Chidsey, Donald Barr. *July 4, 1776*. New York: Crown Publishers, Inc., 1958.

* ———.*Valley Forge*. New York: Crown Publishers, Inc., 1959.

Crawford, Mary Caroline. *Old Boston Days & Ways*. Boston: Little, Brown, and Company, 1909.

Dickerson, Oliver M. *The Navigation Acts and the American Revolution*. Philadelphia: University of Pennsylvania Press, 1951.

Drake, Francis Samuel. *Life and Correspondence of Henry Knox*. Boston: S. G. Drake, 1873.

Drake, Samuel Adams. *Historic Mansions and Highways Around Boston*. New and Revised Edition. Boston: Little, Brown, and Company, 1904.

———. *Old Landmarks and Historic Personages of Boston*. Boston: James R. Osgood and Company, 1872.

Drake, Samuel G. *The History and Antiquities of the City of Boston*. Boston: Luther Stevens, 1854.

Edwards, William Churchill. *Historic Quincy Massaschuetts*. Quincy: Privately printed, 1945.

* Forbes, Esther. *Paul Revere & the World He Lived In*. Boston: Houghton Mifflin Company, 1942.

Friedenwald, Herbert. *The Declaration of Independence: An Interpretation and an Analysis*. New York: The Macmillan Company, 1904.

Frothingham, Richard, Jr. *History of the Siege of Boston, and of the Battles of Lexington, Concord, and Bunker Hill*. Boston: Charles C. Little and James Brown, 1849.

Gilman, Arthur, Editor. *Theatrum Majorum: The Cambridge of 1776*. Cambridge, Mass.: Lockwood, Brooks, and Company, 1876.

Guide Book to the Hancock-Clarke House, Lexington, Massachusetts. Sixth Edition. Lexington, Mass.: Published by the Lexington Historical Society, 1921.

Hazelton, John H. *The Declaration of Independence, Its History*. New York: Dodd, Mead and Company, 1906.

Higginson, Stephen. *Ten Chapters in the Life of John Hancock*. New York: Privately printed, 1857.

Hosmer, James K. *Samuel Adams*. Boston and New York: Houghton, Mifflin and Company, 1885.

Hubbard, Elbert. *Little Journeys to the Homes of American Statesmen*. New York and London: G. P. Putnam's Sons, 1898.

* Lengyel, Cornel. *Four Days in July: The Story Behind the Declaration of Independence*. Garden City, N.Y.: Doubleday & Company, Inc., 1958.

Loring, James Spear. *The Hundred Boston Orators*. Boston: John P. Jewett and Company, 1852.

Lothrop, Samuel Kirkland. *A History of the Church in Brattle Street, Boston*. Boston: Wm. Crosby and H. P. Nichols, 1851.

Malone, Dumas. *The Story of the Declaration of Independence*. New York: Oxford University Press, 1954.

Meigs, Cornelia. *The Violent Men: A Study of the Human Relations in the First American Congress*. New York: The Macmillan Company, 1949.

Miller, John C. *Sam Adams: Pioneer in Propaganda*. Boston: Little, Brown, and Company, 1936.

* Montross, Lynn. *The Reluctant Rebels: The Story of the Continental Congress*. New York: Harper & Brothers, 1950.

Moore, Frank. *Diary of the American Revolution*. 2 vols. New York: Charles Scribner, 1860.

Morison, Samuel Eliot. *Three Centuries of Harvard, 1636-1936*. Cambridge, Mass.: Harvard University Press, 1936.

Musick, John R. *John Hancock: A Character Sketch*. Milwaukee: H. G. Campbell Publishing Company, 1903.

Palfrey, John Gorham. *Life of William Palfrey*. (Vol. XVII in The Library of American Biography, edited by Jared Sparks.) Boston: Charles C. Little and James Brown, 1845.

Parton, James. *Life and Times of Benjamin Franklin*. 2 vols. New York: Mason Bros., 1865.

Pattee, William S. *A History of Old Braintree and Quincy*. Quincy: Green & Prescott, 1878.

Pownall, Charles A. W. *Thomas Pownall*. London: Henry Stevens, Son & Stiles, 1908.

Quincy, Josiah. *The History of Harvard University*. 2 vols. Cambridge, Mass.: John Owen, 1840.

Sabine, Lorenzo. *The American Loyalists*. Boston: Charles C. Little and James Brown, 1847.

Scudder, Townsend. *Concord: American Town*. Boston: Little, Brown and Company, 1947.

Sears, Lorenzo. *John Hancock: The Picturesque Patriot*. Boston: Little, Brown, and Company, 1912.

Shipton, Clifford K. *New England Life in the 18th Century*. Cambridge, Mass.: Harvard University Press, 1963

Shirley, William. *Correspondence of William Shirley*. Edited by

Charles Henry Lincoln. 2 vols. New York: The Macmillan Company, 1912.

Smith, Page. *John Adams.* 2 vols. Garden City, N.Y.: Doubleday & Company, Inc., 1962.

* Tourtellot, Arthur Bernon. *William Diamond's Drum.* Garden City, N.Y.: Doubleday & Company, Inc., 1959.

Ubbelohde, Carl. *The Vice-Admiralty Courts and the American Revolution.* Chapel Hill: The University of North Carolina Press, 1960.

Umbreit, Kenneth. *Founding Fathers: Men Who Shaped Our Tradition.* New York and London: Harper & Brothers, 1941.

* Ward, Christopher. *The War of the Revolution.* Edited by John Richard Alden. 2 vols. New York: The Macmillan Company, 1952.

Watkins, Walter Kendall. "The Hancock House and Its Builder." *Old-Time New England,* July, 1926.

Wells, William V. *The Life and Public Services of Samuel Adams.* 3 vols. Boston: Little, Brown, and Company, 1865.

Whitney, George. *Some Account of the Early History and Present State of the Town of Quincy.* Quincy: Christian Register Office, 1827.

Wilson, Daniel Munro. *Three Hundred Years of Quincy, 1625-1925.* Published by authority of the City Government of Quincy, Massachusetts, 1926.

——. *Where American Independence Began.* Second Edition, Enlarged. Boston and New York: Houghton, Mifflin and Company, 1904.

Winsor, Justin, Editor. *The Memorial History of Boston.* 4 vols. Boston: James R. Osgood and Company, 1881.

Woodbury, Ellen C.D.Q. *Dorothy Quincy, Wife of John Hancock.* Second Edition. Washington and New York: The Neale Publishing Company, 1905.

III. BACKGROUND MATERIAL ON THE COMING OF THE REVOLUTION AND THE ERA OF THE REVOLUTION

Adams, James Truslow. *Revolutionary New England 1691-1776.* Boston: Little, Brown, and Company, 1923.

* Alden, John Richard. *The American Revolution, 1775-1783.* New York: Harper & Brothers, 1954.

* ——. *Rise of the American Republic.* New York, Evanston, and London: Harper & Row, 1963.

Andrews, Charles M. *The Colonial Background of the American Revolution.* New Haven: Yale University Press, 1924.

* Bakeless, John. *Turncoats, Traitors and Heroes.* Philadelphia: J. B. Lippincott and Company, 1959.

Becker, Carl L. *The Declaration of Independence: A Study in the*

History of Political Ideas. Reissue. New York: Alfred A. Knopf, Inc., 1942.

Bemis, Samuel Flagg. *The Diplomacy of the American Revolution.* New York: D. Appleton-Century Co., 1935.

Boswell, James. *Boswell's London Journal, 1762-1763.* With Introduction and Notes by Frederick A. Pottle. New York: McGraw-Hill Book Company, Inc., 1950.

Bridenbaugh, Carl and Jessica. *Rebels and Gentlemen: Philadelphia in the Age of Franklin.* New York: Reynal & Hitchcock, 1942.

Calhoun, Arthur W. *A Social History of the American Family* (Vol. I: *The Colonial Period*). Cleveland: The Arthur H. Clark Company, 1917-1919.

Callahan, North. *Royal Raiders: The Tories of the American Revolution.* Indianapolis and New York: The Bobbs-Merrill Company, Inc., 1963.

Connell, Brian. *The Savage Years.* New York: Harper & Brothers, 1959.

Eliot, Samuel A. *A Sketch of the History of Harvard University.* Boston: Charles C. Little and James Brown, 1848.

French, Allen. *The First Year of the American Revolution.* Boston and New York: Houghton Mifflin Company, 1934.

* Gipson, Lawrence Henry. *The Coming of the Revolution, 1763-1775.* New York: Harper & Brothers, 1954.

* Handlin, Oscar. *The Americans: A New History of the People of the United States.* Boston: Little, Brown and Company, 1963.

Howe, M. A. DeWolfe. *Boston Common: Scenes from Four Centuries.* Boston and New York: Houghton Mifflin Company, 1921.

* Ketchum, Richard M. *The Battle for Bunker Hill.* Garden City, N.Y.: Doubleday & Company, Inc., 1962.

* Lancaster, Bruce. *From Lexington to Liberty.* Garden City, N.Y.: Doubleday & Company, Inc., 1955.

* Lancaster, Bruce, and Plumb, J. H. *The American Heritage Book of the Revolution.* New York: American Heritage Publishing Co., Inc., 1958.

Lossing, Benson J. *The Pictorial Field-Book of the Revolution.* 2 vols. New York: Harper & Brothers, 1855 and 1860.

* Miller, John C. *The Federalist Era, 1789-1801.* New York: Harper & Brothers, 1960.

———. *Origins of the American Revolution.* Boston: Little, Brown and Company, 1943.

Morison, Samuel Eliot. *The Intellectual Life of Colonial New England.* Second Edition. Ithaca, N.Y.: Cornell University Press, 1956.

* Morris, Richard B., Editor. *Encyclopedia of American History.* Revised and Enlarged Edition. New York: Harper & Brothers, 1961.

*Nye, Russel Blaine. *The Cultural Life of the New Nation, 1776-1830*. New York: Harper & Brothers, 1960.

*Perry, Oliver Chitwood. *A History of Colonial America*. Third Edition. New York: Harper & Brothers, 1961.

Scharf, J. Thomas, and Westcott, Thompson. *History of Philadelphia, 1609-1884*. 3 vols. Philadelphia: L. H. Everts Company, 1884.

*Scheer, George F., and Rankin, Hugh F. *Rebels and Redcoats*. Cleveland: The World Publishing Company, 1957.

Schlesinger, Arthur M. *Prelude to Independence: The Newspaper War on Britain, 1764-1776*. New York: Alfred A. Knopf, 1958.

Shackleton, Robert. *The Book of Boston*. Philadelphia: The Penn Publishing Company, 1916.

Singleton, Esther. *Social New York Under the Georges, 1714-1776*. New York: D. Appleton and Company, 1902.

Thacher, James. *Military Journal of the American Revolution*. Hartford: Hurlbut, Williams & Company, 1862. (First published as *A Military Journal During the American Revolutionary War*. Boston, 1823.)

*Tharp, Louise Hall. *The Baroness and the General*. Boston: Little, Brown and Company, 1962.

Turberville, A. S. *English Men and Manners in the Eighteenth Century*. New York: Oxford University Press, 1926.

Vaille, F. O., and Clark, H. A., Editors. *The Harvard Book*. 2 vols. Cambridge, Mass.: Welch, Bigelow, and Company, 1875.

Watson, John F. *Annals of Philadelphia and Pennsylvania in the Olden Times*. 2 vols. Philadelphia: Published by the author, 1844.

Whitehill, Walter Muir. *Boston: A Topographical History*. Cambridge, Mass.: Harvard University Press, 1959.

*Wright, Louis B. *The Cultural Life of the American Colonies, 1607-1763*. New York: Harper & Brothers, 1957.

ADDITIONAL SUGGESTIONS FOR FURTHER READING

Barnes, Eric Wollencott. *Free Men Must Stand: The American War of Independence*. New York: McGraw-Hill Book Company, Inc., 1962.

Boyce, Burke. *Man from Mount Vernon*. New York: Harper & Brothers, 1961.

Chambers, Robert W. *Cardigan*. New York: Harper & Brothers, 1930.

Donovan, Frank R. *The Many Worlds of Benjamin Franklin*. New York: American Heritage Publishing Co., Inc., 1964.

Fisher, Dorothy Canfield. *Paul Revere and the Minute Men*. New York: Random House, 1950.

Forbes, Esther. *Johnny Tremain: A Novel for Old & Young*. Boston: Houghton Mifflin Company, 1943.

Hall-Quest, Olga W. *Guardians of Liberty: Sam Adams and John Hancock*. New York: E. P. Dutton & Company, Inc., 1963.

Kubie, Nora Benjamin. *Joel: A Novel of Young America*. New York: Harper & Brothers, 1952.

McGee, Dorothy Horton. *Famous Signers of the Declaration*. New York: Dodd, Mead & Company, 1955.

Moscow, Henry. *Thomas Jefferson and His World*. New York: American Heritage Publishing Co., Inc., 1960.

Nolan, Jeannette Covert. *The Shot Heard Round the World: The Story of Lexington and Concord*. New York: Julian Messner, Inc., 1963.

Russell, Francis. *The French and Indian Wars*. New York: American Heritage Publishing Co., Inc., 1962.

———. *Lexington, Concord and Bunker Hill*. New York: American Heritage Publishing Co., Inc., 1963.

Speare, Elizabeth George. *Life in Colonial America*. New York: Random House, 1963.

Index

175

About the Author

Born in Philadelphia, raised in Moorestown and Haddonfield, New Jersey, Frederick Wagner received his M.A. degree from Duke University and then taught English at the University of Oklahoma and at Duke. After a stint in the army during the Korean conflict, he came to New York City. He is now promotion manager for a major book publisher.

Writing about Mr. Wagner's *Famous Underwater Adventurers* in the *New York Times Book Review*, Henry W. Hubbard, science editor of *Newsweek*, said, "He is certainly a good storyteller. His tales are vivid, humorous and informative. The more sophisticated reader will get special enjoyment from the author's gentle nuances and wry twists and learn a great deal, too."

Best Sellers described his biography of David Bushnell, *Submarine Fighter of the American Revolution*, as "a fascinating story for readers of every age. In his work the author reaches the happy medium of easy style and scholarly research, producing a work which is at one time historically accurate and highly literary in quality."

With his wife, Barbara Brady, Frederick Wagner is the co-author of *Famous American Actors and Actresses*, a volume which George Freedley, President, Theatre Library Association, has called "invaluable."